1   Introduction

In the decade since John B. Taylor's celebrated essay on "Discretion versus policy rules in practice" was presented at the 39th Carnegie-Rochester Conference on Public Policy in the Fall of 1992, his analysis has had considerable influence on the way monetary economists and practitioners think about the policy debate. Taylor showed that actual monetary policy in the United States could be usefully described in terms of a simple rule that appeared promising on the basis of policy evaluation experiments. Most importantly, he described the monetary policy process in terms of the short-term nominal interest rate that was close to the actual decision making process, and described policy directly in terms of the two major operational objectives of monetary policy, inflation and economic growth.

My aim in this study is to investigate the usefulness of the Taylor-rule framework as an organizing device for describing the policy debate and evolution of monetary policy in the United States. Key to this undertaking is the examination of interest rate policy decisions linked directly to the Federal Reserve's underlying policy objectives, as these may have been understood over time. In the spirit of Friedman and Schwartz (1963), I rely heavily on narrative descriptions of events and ideas, supplemented, as possible, with information available to policy practitioners when policy was made. A major difference is my reliance on the language of interest-rate-based policies, instead of the stock of money, and some of the resulting analysis can be seen as a re-interpretation of earlier findings using the latter language. The ultimate goal of this effort is to use the historical experience to draw lessons about past policy successes and policy errors.

The theme that emerges from this examination is that Federal Reserve policies over many periods, virtually since the founding of the institution, can be broadly interpreted in terms of the Taylor-rule framework with surprising consistency. The Taylor rule serves as a particularly good description of policy, however, both when subsequent economic outcomes were exemplary as well as less than ideal. A recurrent source of errors has been misperceptions of the state of the economy, the result of incorrect assessments of the economy's productive potential. This concept has appeared in policy discussions with different names and in various contexts from the first years of operation of the System. It has often led to false predictions of inflation or disinflation, prompting tightening or easing actions that were only recognized as counterproductive long after the fact. This historical analysis suggests that the Taylor rule appears to serve as a useful organizing device for interpreting past policy decisions and mistakes, but adoption of the Taylor-rule framework for policy analysis is not insurance that past policy mistakes would not have occured.

2 Two Interpretations of the Taylor Rule

In his original exposition of a rule-based framework for monetary policy analysis, Taylor offered two interpretations of rules-based policy. The first concentrated on an example presented with a precise algebraic formula. The second emphasized the broad characteristics of policy rules, recognizing that, as with virtually any rule, implementation details should be left to policymakers. Although the precise algebraic formula caught most of the attention originally, my analysis suggests that the broader interpretation is of at least as much interest, especially for historical analysis. In this section, I review the two interpretations, and relate the framework to an alternative simple rule motivated by money growth targeting.

2.1 A Narrow Interpretation: The Classic Taylor Rule

The specific example that captivated so much attention was presented by Taylor as a "hypothetical but representative policy rule" (1993, p. 214). In effect, this example was a particular parameterization of a policy rule that had already been studied in detail by participants of the Brookings project on policy regime evaluation reported in Bryant, Hooper and Mann (1993), and also examined in another contribution to the Fall 1992 Carnegie-Rochester conference by Henderson and McKibbin (1993).[1] The Brookings study examined rules setting deviations of the short-term nominal interest, i, from a baseline path, i^*, in proportion to deviations of a target variables z, from its target, z^*.

$$i - i^* = \theta(z - z^*) \tag{1}$$

Among the alternative target variables examined, the collective findings in the Brookings study pointed to two as more likely to result in better economic performance. One of

---

[1] The Brookings conference, which took place in March 1990, and to which both Taylor, and Henderson and McKibbin contributed, appears to have had an influence on the contributions by Taylor and by Henderson and McKibbin to the 1992 Carnegie-Rochester conference. Taylor's contribution on nominal GNP targeting at an earlier Carnegie-Rochester conference (Taylor 1985), offered an earlier related analysis of some of the issues that also appeared in the later work.

these suggested targeting the sum of the price level p, and real output q—that is nominal income, $p+q$ ("nominal income targeting regime"). The other suggested targeting the sum of inflation, $\pi = \Delta p$, and real output ("real-output-plus-inflation targeting regime"):[2]

$$i - i^* = \theta((\pi + q) - (\pi^* + q^*)) \tag{2}$$

Variations of this formulation, with differential responses to inflation and output:

$$i - i^* = \theta_\pi(\pi - \pi^*) + \theta_q(q - q^*) \tag{3}$$

were also considered in some of the contributions to the Brookings study. In his parameterization, Taylor adopted the "real-output-plus-inflation" variant and set the baseline nominal interest rate to equal the sum of the equilibrium or natural rate of interest, r^*, and inflation, π. He employed an output gap measure obtained from a smooth trend, $y = q - q^*$, and used the year-over-year rate of change of the output deflator to measure inflation. Setting the inflation target and equilibrium real interest equal to two and the response parameter, θ to one half, he arrived at what we now know as the classic Taylor rule:

$$i = 2 + \pi + \frac{1}{2}(\pi - 2) + \frac{1}{2}(q - q^*) \tag{4}$$

Taylor noted that this parameterization appeared to fit Federal Reserve behavior well over the previous several years and observed: "If the policy rule comes so close to describing actual Federal Reserve behavior in recent years and if FOMC members believe that such performance was good and should be replicated in the future even under a different set of circumstances, then a policy rule could provide some guidance to future decisions." (p. 208.)

2.2   Some Limitations

Some of the suggested attractive qualities of this rule, however, were promptly questioned. As McCallum (1993) noted, Taylor's formulation was not "operational." It required information that the policymaker did not necessarily have at his disposal.[3] Crucially, this formula requires policymakers to take a stand on and formulate policy on the basis of implicit

---

[2]Unless otherwise noted, I use capital letters to denote levels and small letters (except for interest rates) to denote respective logarithms. Throughout, I use log differences to approximate rates of change, scaled to annual rates, in percent. Interest rates are in percent, annual rates.

[3]McCallum was originally concerned with the timing of information on inflation and the output gap. Orphanides (2001, 2003) later demonstrated that the informational problem was broader and quantitatively severe in practice, especially regarding the measurement of the "output gap."

assumptions regarding concepts such as the natural rate of interest and potential output (or the related natural rate of unemployment or "NAIRU"), which are known to be notoriously unreliable as policy indicators.[4] Not all academic observers and policy practitioners believe such concepts are either necessary or helpful for formulating policy. Policymakers, in particular, might prefer to avoid the dogmatic reliance on natural-rate-gap-based policy rules, such as Taylor's classic formulation.[5]

At the very least, these difficulties serve as an important reason for viewing this particular rule as a strategy that could only be implemented with a substantial element of discretion. This point was emphasized by Chairman Greenspan in 1997:

> As Taylor himself has pointed out, these types of formulations are at best "guideposts" to help central banks, not inflexible rules that eliminate discretion. One reason is that their formulation depends on the values of certain key variables– most crucially the equilibrium real federal funds rate and the production potential of the economy. In practice these have been obtained by observation of past macroeconomic behavior–either through informal inspection of the data, or more formally as embedded in models. In that sense, like all rules, as I noted earlier, they embody a forecast that the future will be like the past. Unfortunately, however, history is not an infallible guide to the future, and the levels of these two variables are currently under active debate.

In addition, the classic Taylor rule lacks an explicit role for forecasts and related judgments about prospective economic developments. As noted by Meyer (2002):

> Although the Taylor rule has been a useful benchmark for policymakers, my experience during the last 5-1/2 years on the FOMC has been that considerations that are not explicit in the Taylor rule have played an important role in policy deliberations. In particular, forecasts clearly have played a powerful role in shaping the response of monetary policy in a way not reflected in the simple Taylor rule.

Indeed, forecasts of the economic outlook have always served an important role in monetary policy decisions at the Federal Reserve, with rather similar justifications being provided for

---

[4]Quantifications of this unreliability are presented in several recent studies, including Staiger, Stock and Watson (1997), and Laubach (2001), for the natural rate of unemployment; Christiano and Fitzgerald (2001), Orphanides and van Norden (2002), and van Norden (2002) for potential output; Laubach and Williams (2001), for the natural rate of interest and Orphanides and Williams (2002), for the natural rates of interest and unemployment.

[5]The classic exposition of the dangers of such natural-rate-gap-based policies appears in Friedman's 1967 AEA presidential address, (Friedman, 1968).

this practice over the decades. Consider, for instance, the following remarks by Chairman Greenspan from 1999 and the remarks by Chairman Martin in 1965, both offered during periods when monetary policy was in a tightening phase and inflation appeared to be the predominant threat.

> For monetary policy to foster maximum sustainable economic growth, it is useful to preempt forces of imbalance before they threaten economic stability. But this may not always be possible—the future at times can be too opaque to penetrate. When we can be preemptive, we should be, because modest preemptive actions can obviate more drastic actions at a later date that would destabilize the economy. (Greenspan, 1999)

> To me, the effective time to act against inflationary pressures is when they are in the development stage—before they have become full-blown and the damage has been done. Precautionary measures are more likely to be effective than remedial action: the old proverb that an ounce of prevention is worth a pound of cure applies to monetary policy as well as to anything else. (Martin, 1965)

More generally, preemption appeared to be a guiding principle of the Federal Reserve as early as the founding of the System. As the Board explained in its *First Annual Report for 1914*, which was published in January 1915: "[A reserve bank's] duty is not to await emergencies but by anticipation, to do what it can to prevent them."

Given that Federal Reserve officials have always described the formulation of monetary policy as a forward-looking process, policy rules failing to incorporate such information into historical analyses of policy decisions could easily prove inadequate. A popular approach is to modify Taylor's classic formulation by replacing current and recent outcomes in rules of the form (3) with forecasts of these variables.[6] Alternatively, as suggested by Taylor (1993), policymakers could consult the forecast path of the federal funds rate obtained by projecting rule (3) using forecasts of inflation and economic activity. Attempting to incorporate an explicit role for forecasts in a monetary policy rule, however, must be seen in the context of a broader interpretation of policy rules than the one embedded in Taylor's classic rule example. I turn to such a broad interpretation next.

---

[6]Examples of such variants in policy evaluations and descriptive exercises include Batini and Haldane (1999), Batini and Nelson (2000), Clarida, Gali and Gertler (1999, 2000), Levin, Wieland and Williams (1999, 2003), Nessen (1999) and Orphanides (2001, 2002, 2003).

2.3 A Broad Interpretation

The broad interpretation of Taylor's rule-based framework for monetary policy provides a degree of flexibility that addresses some of the perceived limitations of the classic rule. In describing this broad interpretation Taylor stressed that "a policy rule need not be a mechanical formula," (1993, p. 198). Rather, adopting a position closer to earlier interpretations of policy rules such as in Samuelson (1951, 1967) and Tobin (1983), Taylor emphasized the broader definition of a rule as a systematic policy program geared towards the attainment of the fundamental policy objectives. In general terms, Taylor described the fundamental features of the policy he was proposing by quoting a useful summary description from the 1990 *Economic Report of the President*, (which, as a member of the Council that year, he had co-authored):

> The Federal Reserve generally increases interest rates when inflationary pressures appear to be rising and lowers interest rates when inflationary pressures are abating and recession appears to be more of a threat. (Council of Economic Advisers, 1990, p. 85).

As with the classic, narrow interpretation, the objectives of monetary policy are to dampen business cycle fluctuations and maintain price stability. But unlike the narrow interpretation, policymakers are given more leeway in taking actions to achieve the desired effect. This permits the use of sound judgment outside the scope of any fixed formula in formulating policy and without restricting policymakers necessarily to a specific analytical framework.

Of course, this broad interpretation has the disadvantage of reduced precision—indeed as a policy rule it must be seen as one whose implementation *requires* discretion. On the other hand, this broad interpretation of Taylor's rule-based policy presents some substantial advantages as a descriptive device. It maintains a role for pre-emption and the use of forecasts in setting policy, and it accommodates the exhibited policymakers' preference for adopting explicitly forward-looking policy guides. Equally important, Taylor's broad interpretation does not require policymakers to accept natural-rate-gap-based policy as their guiding principle. By being more encompassing, the broad interpretation of the Taylor rule arguably better captures the actual policy process over time.

This broad interpretation of Taylor's framework, as opposed to the classic Taylor rule, also relates more closely to the inflation targeting approach to policy, discussed in Bernanke and Mishkin (1997), and Bernanke, Laubach, Mishkin and Posen (1998). Indeed, as Bernanke and Mishkin stress, inflation targeting is a framework of "constrained discretion."

The broader interpretation of Taylor's policy framework places its emphasis on the identification of the System's *operational* objectives regarding price stability and economic growth and asks that policymakers apply their collective judgment to adjust interest rates so as to balance the perceived risks with regard to the outlook for the two objectives. In this sense, the crucial element for interpreting historical monetary policy with the Taylor rule rests on two elements: First, the extent to which the System has relied on short-term interest rates as its primary policy instrument, which is widely accepted as a fairly accurate description. Second, the evolution of the System's operational objectives vis-a-vis price stability and economic growth, as interpreted by policymakers over time for the conduct of policy. As I illustrate next, policymaking in the System has broadly exhibited a remarkable consistency in this regard as well. The System's consistency with regard to these two key elements of the Taylor-rule framework through time provides the strongest rationale for the usefulness of the framework for interpreting historical monetary policy decisions.

2.4 Policy Objectives and Strategy Over Time

An appropriate starting point for examining the evolution of policy objectives and their interpretation is to examine the current statutory objectives of the System, as reflected in the November 16, 1977 amendment of Section 2A of the Federal Reserve Act. These are: "maximum employment, stable prices, and moderate long-term interest rates." A recent operational interpretation can be found in the Committee's January 19, 2000 statement which introduced the practice of announcing: "the FOMC's consensus about the balance of risks to the attainment of its long-run goals of price stability and sustainable economic growth." Related interpretations of the dual objective of price stability and maximum growth can be traced back to the legislative mandate of the Employment Act of 1946. As an illustration, consider the following statement from a 1957 Congressional Hearing:

> The objective of the System is always the same—to promote monetary and credit conditions that will foster sustained economic growth together with stability in the value of the dollar. (United States Congress, 1957, p. 1252.)

However, even before the 1946 Act, the Federal Reserve appeared to be interpreting its "implicit" objectives in rather similar terms. The following statement from *the Annual Report for 1945* suggests a modern interpretation of both the goals of policy, as well as the broad guiding principles for Taylor's conduct of policy:

> It is the Board's belief that the implicit predominant purpose of Federal Reserve policy is to contribute, insofar as the limitations of monetary and credit policy permit, to an economic environment favorable to the highest possible degree of sustained production and employment. Traditionally, this over-all policy has been followed by easing credit conditions when deflationary factors prevailed and, conversely, by restricting measures when inflationary forces threatened.

Indeed, as Chairman McCabe noted in 1949: "... for the entire period since 1935, Federal Reserve credit policies have been altogether in conformity with the objectives stated in the Employment Act of 1946. Review of a longer period would show that throughout the System's existence Federal Reserve objectives have been in harmony with these broad purposes." (Joint Committee on the Economic Report, 1949, p. 25-26.)

2.5 Monetary Growth Targeting in the Taylor Framework

The broad interpretation of the Taylor rule is also of interest because it permits investigations of alternative specific policy rules that are consistent with the attainment of the policy objectives of price stability and maximum sustainable growth.

One such example may be viewed as a reformulation of Friedman's monetary growth rule in terms of the family of policy rules investigated in the Brookings study. Recall that one of the key advantages of Friedman's money growth rule is that is stays clear of the pitfalls known to plague the natural-rate-gap-based policy approach. In terms of rule (1), a strategy that meets this criterion but maintains the spirit of the "nominal income" and "real-output-plus-inflation" targeting regimes considered in the Brookings project, is to set the *growth* (instead of the level) of nominal income, $\Delta(p+q) = \pi + \Delta q$, as the target variable z, and rely on the lagged value of the interest rate instrument as the baseline for policy adjustments. The resulting rule becomes:

$$\Delta i = \theta((\pi + \Delta q) - (\pi^* + \Delta q^*)) \tag{5}$$

To see the relationship to money growth targeting recall that, given a monetary aggregate,

m, and its velocity, v, the equation of exchange implies:

$$\Delta m + \Delta v = \pi + \Delta q \qquad (6)$$

Allowing for adjustments in the change of equilibrium velocity and potential output growth, a non-activist money growth rule with the objective of achieving an inflation target π^* sets:[7]

$$\Delta m = \pi^* + \Delta q^* - \Delta v^* \qquad (7)$$

or, after substituting the equation of exchange, stated in terms of velocity:

$$\Delta v - \Delta v^* = (\pi - \pi^*) + (\Delta q - \Delta q^*) \qquad (8)$$

To reformulate this strategy in terms of an interest rate rule, consider the simplest formulation of money demand as a (log-) linear relationship between velocity deviations from its equilibrium and the rate of interest. In difference form this is:[8]

$$\Delta v - \Delta v^* = a\Delta i + e \qquad (9)$$

where $a > 0$ and e summarizes short-run dynamics and money-demand fluctuations. Substituting (9) into (8) but without the term e—that is avoiding the short-run velocity fluctuations which are the suggested principal drawback of money growth strategies that interest-rate based strategies are designed to avoid—yields:

$$\Delta i = \theta((\pi - \pi^*) + (\Delta q - \Delta q^*)) \qquad (10)$$

where $\theta > 0$. As can be readily seen, this has exactly the same form as rule (5). More generally, money growth rules that incorporate additional responses to inflation, real output

---

[7]For example, Friedman's famous 4% rule for the growth of M2 during the late 1960s and early 1970s, corresponded to a zero inflation target with the assumptions that M2 velocity exhibited no trend and potential output growth equaled 4% (the prevailing estimate at the time), or with the assumption of a somewhat smaller estimate of potential output growth and a corresponding small downward trend in velocity.

[8]This reformulation presupposes that interest rates are positive and not near the zero bound. If additional monetary easing is required when the rate is at zero, it can be easily achieved by increasing the rate of money growth further, but this easing is obviously not reflected in additional reductions in the interest rate policy instrument. This break in the link between interest rates and easy money sometimes leads to the flawed conclusion that no additional easing is possible at the zero bound. (Examples would be the experience during the Great Depression and, more recently, in Japan. See Orphanides, 2003d, for details.) As Taylor stressed at a 1995 Bank of Japan conference, the deflation experienced at the time in Japan "made an interest rate rule unreliable, calling for greater emphasis on money supply rules." (Taylor 1997, p. 36). Orphanides and Wieland (2000) elaborate on this transition from Taylor-rule-based to money-based policies under these circumstances. Using data from the Great Depression and recent Japanese experience, they also illustrate how the simple velocity-interest rate relationship reflected in (9) breaks down at the zero bound.

growth or nominal output growth, such as rules in the spirit of Brunner, Cooper, Fischer, McCallum and Meltzer, which can be written as:[9]

$$\Delta m = \pi^* + \Delta q^* - \Delta v^* - b_\pi(\pi - \pi^*) - b_{\Delta q}(\Delta q - \Delta q^*) \tag{11}$$

for $b_\pi, b_{\Delta q} \geq 0$ can be similarly reformulated as

$$\Delta i = \theta_\pi(\pi - \pi^*) + \theta_{\Delta q}(\Delta q - \Delta q^*) \tag{12}$$

for positive values of θ_π and $\theta_{\Delta q}$. To differentiate these specific rules from Taylor's classic formulation, I will refer to them as natural-growth targeting rules to highlight that these rules rely on estimates of the economy's natural growth rate for guidance, responding to perceived imbalances between the growth of aggregate demand and aggregate supply, and not an output gap.[10]

In words, these natural-growth targeting rules call for the Federal Reserve to raise interest rates "when inflationary pressures appear to be rising" and lower rates "when inflationary pressures are abating and recession appears to be more of a threat," matching quite closely Taylor's verbal description of the broad guidelines for an interest-rate-based rule described earlier. Indeed, Taylor himself stressed the broad relation of money growth targeting rules and his interest-rate-based policy framework (1993, p. 209 and 1999, p. 322) and also suggested "a policy rule where the growth rate of GDP rather than its level appears" (1993, p. 208) as one of the examples of specific rules that Federal Reserve staff could present to the FOMC as part of the policy decision process.[11] The reliance of information regarding growth rates, as opposed to natural-rate gaps, is also not inconsistent with verbal descriptions of policy considerations.[12] As with Taylor's classic alternative, natural-growth

---

[9]Brunner and Meltzer (1993), Cooper and Fischer (1972, 1974), Fischer and Cooper (1973), Meltzer (1987), McCallum (1988, 1990, 2000).

[10]Rules (10) and (12) also relate to price level targeting and to nominal income targeting rules, stated in difference form. Letting $n = \pi + \Delta q$ denote the growth of nominal income and $n^* = \pi^* + \Delta q^*$ denote the natural growth of nominal income, given the desired rate of inflation, the simplest form, (10), can be written more simply as: $\Delta i = \theta(n - n^*)$. Orphanides and Williams (2002) offer detailed econometric policy evaluation comparisons of rules of the form (3) and (12) and an extensive bibliography of earlier studies examining the relative merits of the level/difference elements of the two alternatives. See, in particular, Goodfriend (1991), Levin et al (1999), Rotemberg and Woodford (1999), Sack and Wieland (2000), Williams (1999) and Woodford (1999) for the role of interest smoothing and Leitemo and Lonning (2001), McCallum (2001), Orphanides et al (2000), Woodford (2002), and Walsh (2003) for the role of output growth.

[11]McCallum (2000) and Razzak (2003) also investigated the relation between money-growth and interest-rate-based policy rules. A grandparent of such comparisons is the classic study by Poole (1970).

[12]A recent example to this effect appeared in remarks by Chairman Greenspan articulating his concerns

targeting rules could be implemented based on either current data and recent realizations of inflation and output growth, or based on the outlook of inflation and growth in the near future.

3 Monetary Policy Since the Treasury-Federal Reserve Accord Through the Lens of a Taylor Rule

Figure 1 provides a summary overview of macroeconomic developments in the United States since 1951—the year that marked the re-birth of the System following the subordination of Federal Reserve policy to Treasury financing operations during World War II.[13] The top panel shows the familiar path of inflation, measured as the rate of change of the output (GDP) deflator over four quarters. The middle panel plots real output growth over four quarters (solid line) as well as an estimate of the natural rate of growth of the economy over time—the growth of potential output (dotted line). The bottom panel plots an estimate of the output gap. All data in the figure are the most recently available estimates, as produced by the Commerce Department for the GDP data and by the Congressional Budget Office for potential output. As is well known, all of these series, but particularly the estimates of potential output, are subject to revisions, redefinitions, rebenchmarks, remodeling and so forth—an issue whose significance will become evident shortly. In this, and subsequent figures, the vertical dotted lines represent business cycle peaks and troughs as dated by the National Bureau of Economic Research (NBER). (The narrow spacing reflects peaks and the wide spacing troughs, respectively. As of this writing, the date of the trough of the recession that started in 2001 has not been announced.)

Historical policy evaluation is seen as an attempt to explain the interactions of policy decision with subsequent economic outcomes, and to assess whether policy action or inaction was appropriate in terms of its direction, timing and perhaps magnitude. The most precise method for such evaluations requires the use of a model. Such evaluations, however, are limited by and the results are conditioned upon the confidence with which we can hold that the model serves as an adequate representation of reality for that purpose. Given our

---

about the economic outlook in January 2000, during a tightening policy phase: "It is this imbalance between growth of supply and growth of demand that contains the potential seeds of rising inflationary and financial pressures that could undermine the current expansion."

[13]Hetzel and Leach (2001) provide a fascinating narrative account of the events leading to the March 4, 1951 Accord.

severely limited knowledge of the workings of the economy, we can therefore never hope to be able to evaluate specific actions with much accuracy, even in hindsight. We may, however, succeed in pinpointing particular periods when better outcomes would appear to have been likely, at least with the benefit of hindsight, had better policies been pursued. For example, retrospectively, it is sometimes straightforward to identify periods when the economy was overheated and inflation was deviating from price stability. Based on just rudimentary knowledge of the monetary transmission mechanism and its lags, those are periods *before* which tighter monetary policy would have been seen as more successful than its actual path. Consider, for instance, the years surrounding 1955, 1965, 1978—to select just an example from each of the first three decades shown. In each case, according to the figure, output exceeded its potential, output growth exceeded the growth of potential supply, and inflation worsened. In each case, if an outside observer to the System could have rerun that particular episode in history (with the benefit of hindsight), tighter monetary policy would have likely been suggested.

In general, for a suggested monetary policy framework to be seen as an improvement over the arrangements that in fact were put in place over history, it must be the case that the framework would have suggested a better policy, at least over some of these clearly identifiable periods, and no worse policy at most other times. Accurate identification of any suggested improvement, however, requires that policy rule prescriptions from a rule under consideration be based on information available to policymakers when decisions are made, as opposed to information that has become available ex post. This distinction is of particular significance for natural-rate-gap-based policy rules as natural rate concepts are particularly prone to revision on the basis of the subsequent evolution of the economy, which is obviously unknown when policy decisions are made.

In this section, I conduct counterfactual analyses of the Taylor rule over the past half century examining the performance of such strategies with the criteria outlined above. To illustrate the dangers of historical evaluation that is not based on real-time information, I build on the approach I suggested in earlier work (2000, 2001, 2003c) and distinguish between real-time and retrospective renditions of history, as seen through the lens of Taylor rules. To that end, I perform parallel exercises using the two alternative information environments.

3.1 The Classic Taylor Rule Over the Past Twenty Years.

Some key issues regarding the distinction between real-time and retrospective analysis can be usefully highlighted by reconstructing the classic rendition of the Taylor rule, as it was originally published. Figure 2 plots alternative versions of the classic Taylor rule against the federal funds rate since mid-1982. The solid line in the figure shows the evolution of the federal funds rate during this period. The dark dashed line (the "1992" rule) reconstructs the Taylor rule as was originally published, replicating all of Taylor's original assumptions. The two vertical lines mark the beginning and end of the sample over which the rule was originally examined, from 1987:1 to 1992:4.[14]

Comparison of the 1992 version of the rule and actual policy confirms Taylor's finding that this simple rule matched the actual behavior of policy in the 1987:1 to 1992:4 remarkably well. However, as can be seen in the figure, this match did not extend to earlier years, even using Taylor's original data and assumptions. To extend the rule forward, I also constructed a "2002" rendition of the rule. For this exercise, I rely on the latest published data, as shown in Figure 1.[15] The resulting rule prescriptions using rule (3), that is maintaining the implicit assumptions $r^* = \pi^* = 2$, is shown with the thin-wide-dash line in the figure. The classic version of the Taylor rule based on the latest data does not appear particularly impressive as a description of policy over the past twenty years. Of course, neither the 1992 nor the 2002 renditions reflect actual policy settings that policymakers following rule (3) could have arrived at in real time. Rather, as output data and estimates of potential output undergo continuous revisions, to recover those realistic settings requires a reconstruction of the real-time rendition of the rule. For this, extending forward the data presented in Orphanides (2001, 2003) I created a dataset with first announced measures of output data and real-time estimates of potential output, as would be available to the FOMC at the time of the FOMC meetings by the middle month of any quarter. Federal Reserve staff estimates for quarters after 1997:4 are not yet available to the public and could not be used

---

[14]Data for the 1992:4 quarter were not available at the time of the 1992 conference given Taylor's use of within-quarter data for forming prescriptions for his rule but became available before publication of the original study. For this replication, I rely on data as available in 1993:1, which also match closely the figures in Taylor (1993), the published version of the paper.

[15]Thus, for the "2002" rendition shown, the output gap is defined using the CBO estimates of potential output. The CBO series has also been employed over the past few years by the Federal Reserve Bank of St Louis for illustrations of the Taylor rule published in the monthly publication *Monetary Trends*.

for this study, however. To complete this dataset, I relied on the real-time CBO estimates for the past five years instead.[16] (These estimates are published twice a year, usually in February and August). Finally, to avoid the use of within-quarter forecasts in creating the real-time rendition of the rule, I adopted the operational version of the classic Taylor rule in this real-time reconstruction. That is, in each quarter t, the output gap and inflation data inputs to the rule are for those for quarter $t-1$. (Data for quarter $t-1$ are the most recent available actual data during quarter t.) The result is shown with the dotted line. The contours of the real-time rule do not capture the contours of policy quite as well as the "1992" rendition. The real-time rendition tracks policy well only in a few of the years of Taylor's sample.

An obvious difficulty is that the real-time rule as well as the "2002" rendition yield prescriptions that appear too low, on average, even for the period originally examined by Taylor. An important problem, which generates this average discrepancy, is that alternative historical renditions of the underlying series for inflation and, particularly, for the output gap, may have different averages for any given period. Variations in these averages, in turn, suggest that alternative assumptions regarding the equilibrium real interest rate would be required to reconcile the stance of a rule with either actual policy, or policy desired to achieve a specific operational objective for inflation *on average*. Unfortunately, since the appropriate *averages* cannot be known at the time policy is made, real-time renditions of the classic Taylor rule may provide policy prescriptions that are systematically too tight or too easy for extended periods of time. Needless to say, this is not a problem if our main interest is simply to find a rule that appears to "fit" policy ex post. We can always choose assumptions to ensure the correct averages—though the interpretation of the resulting "fitted" rule is not clear in such an exercise. However, this is a problem of great significance if the aim is to identify a specific rule meant to be useful for real-time policy analysis.

3.2 Moving Backwards in Time

Figure 3 provides a real-time comparison with the retrospective view of the economy presented in Figure 1 from 1951 to the present. The data are shifted by one quarter, so that

---

[16] Obviously, without knowing whether and how closely these real-time estimates reflect the parallel real-time estimates at the Federal Reserve, rule prescriptions based on these estimates should not be interpreted as necessarily bearing a resemblance to actual rule prescriptions that could have presumably been produced at the Federal Reserve in real time.

observations plotted in quarter t reflect values for quarter $t-1$. This is done to capture the one-quarter lag with which initial estimates of actual output data have generally become available during this period. The real-time data in the figure are also limited to the period after 1960, reflecting the beginning of the systematic construction of potential GNP/GDP in the United States and the availability of quarterly real output data. Thus, for the 1950s, the estimates shown for the real-time output gap series are based on Okun's (1962) quarterly estimates—the published version of the estimates originally presented in Heller, Gordon and Tobin (1961).[17] From 1961:1 to 1979:4, the data on potential output reflect the Council of Economic Advisers estimates, which, as detailed in Orphanides (2000, 2003, 2003c), represented the "official" estimates during this period and were widely used, including by the staff at the Federal Reserve. (Board staff first presented output gap estimates based on these data to the FOMC at the June 1961 FOMC meeting.) As highlighted in Figure 3, real-time perceptions of the state of the economy over this period at times differed markedly from current perceptions. Revisions in the inflation and real output growth data have at times been significant, even exceeding one percentage point. Most problematic, retrospectively, appear to have been estimates of the output gap and their revisions. Part of these revisions can be attributed to revisions in the measurement of *actual* output.[18] In general, however, the most problematic element associated with real-time estimates of the output gap is that it is based on end-of-sample estimates of an output trend (potential output), which are unavoidably highly imprecise. Statistical techniques and models employed for estimating potential output have evolved during this period, reflecting, among other elements, the evolution of best accepted estimation practice.[19] This complicates the

---

[17]To be sure, estimates of *potential* GNP were generated in earlier years, dating as far back as the time when estimates of *actual* GNP first appeared. But prior to the 1960s, their construction was not as systematic and relied on annual data. Quarterly data on real output, were introduced in December 1958 (United States Department of Commerce, 1958). The earliest estimates of potential GNP published by the Federal Reserve Board, as far as I have been able to determine, are those presented in the May 1944 *Bulletin* (Goldenweiser and Hagen, 1944). In light of the later discussion, it is of interest to note that these estimates presumed that an unemployment rate of 3.3 percent corresponded to the non-inflationary full employment potential for the economy.

[18]As shown in the middle panel, revisions in the measurement of real output growth were unusually large and one sided around 1975. For that year, as much as five percentage points of the revision in the output gap could be attributed to the revisions in the real-time estimates of output growth (Orphanides, 2000).

[19]Of course, over history, best accepted practices and most fashionable theories proclaiming to identify the "optimal" approach of the day need not correspond to and may vary greatly from what one might consider best practices at later times. With the benefit of hindsight, and based on later methodological perspectives, one can always identify flaws, false starts, and recurrent periods of regress.

interpretation of the total revision presented in the figure.[20] An important commonality, however, is that throughout this period estimates of potential output were meant to correspond to a concept of non-inflationary (or non-increasing-inflation) level of employment and production. For example, in constructing the earliest of the real-time estimates shown in the figure (in 1961:1) Okun emphasized: "The full employment goal must be understood as striving for maximum production without inflation pressure" (Okun, 1962, p. 82). Thus, these estimates reflect real-time perceptions of the *non-inflationary* productive potential of the economy, and the evolution of these perceptions over time. Real-time perceptions and retrospective "reality," needless to say, proved to be far apart for long stretches over this sample.

The effect of the historical revisions in inflation and the output gap on policy prescriptions from the classic Taylor rule are shown in Figure 4. The figure plots two renditions (real-time and retrospective) of the operational version of the rule (with data lagged by a quarter, as shown in Figure 3) with the original assumptions $\pi^* = r^* = 2$.

Consider again the years 1955, 1965 and 1978. On these three occasions, based on the current rendition of the data, policy prescribed by the rule would have been tighter than actual decisions. However, as a comparison with the real-time rendition of the rule makes clear, the stance of policy adopted by the FOMC during these three years was either about as tight (in 1955 and 1978) or tighter than would have been suggested by the rule (in 1965). The primary difference is that for all three years current estimates indicate that the economy was overheated, while at the time this overheating was not as clear.

In 1955, real-time information indicated the economy may have been on the verge of achieving and perhaps exceeding full capacity, based on perceptions at the time. The policy record points to an awareness of the difficulties of assessing the limits of expansion and the Committee's intent to act pre-emptively in the face of threats of an overheated economy.[21] But policymakers at the time did not recognize the extent of the inflationary danger reflected

---

[20]Orphanides and van Norden (2002) present decompositions of sources of errors in estimation of output gap estimates based on various fixed statistical techniques from the mid-1960s to the late-1990s. Their results suggest that the statistical properties of the revisions shown here are not out of line with those of revisions corresponding to many statistical techniques, even if a common technique had been used over time. Needless to say, ignorance as to which method is "the best" is one of the fundamental issues regarding estimation of *any* natural rate concept, including the level of potential output.

[21]These positive elements of policy during the 1950s are not always appreciated, a point emphasized recently by Romer and Romer (2002) who argue that policy during that period was more modern that is frequently presumed.

in current data. In a sense, they appeared to have the wrong sign on the gap—although the level of utilization of resources was not nearly as important an indicator as it became later, following the perceived methodological advancements for policy control during the 1960s.[22] Consider the following descriptions of the economic situation and need for action from the *Minutes* for the August 2, 1955, FOMC meeting:[23]

> I do not know whether we have reached the limits of our productive capacity in terms of men, materials and equipment. On these matters we have opinions rather than conclusive evidence. (Sproul statement, p. 21.)

> We can all agree that the economic situation is ebullient and presses on the comfortable capacity of the economy. It can thus be concluded that the apparent present trends in the economy simply extend themselves to over-reach comfortable capacity and that, accordingly, an inflation is inevitable in the absence of additional immediate, and substantial monetary restraint. (Bryan statement, p. 23.)

> Inflation is a thief in the night and if we don't act promptly and decisively we will always be behind. All of us know that it sometimes takes a long time for seeds to germinate, but when they flower, they do so with explosive force. (Martin, p 13)

The Committee decided to tighten policy, but given the easy money policy that was earlier in place, a bout of inflation, evident in the top panel of Figure 3, could not be averted.

In 1965, the economy was believed to be approaching full capacity for the first time since the close monitoring of output gap measures had begun four years earlier. By contrast, as seen in Figure 3, according to the current CBO estimates the economy was already severely overheated. But again, the extent of the danger was not recognized in time, despite (or perhaps because of) a forward-looking "modern" framework.[24] Although, retrospectively,

---

[22]The statement regarding the sign of the gap presupposes that the 1961 estimate of potential output for 1955 used in the figure is similar to prevailing perceptions in 1955. This appears consistent with narrative evidence from the period.

[23]One of the critical pieces of new information at this meeting was a revision to the NIPA for the previous 3 years which both significantly dampened the depth of the 1953-54 recession and raised estimates of growth during the subsequent expansion. This prompted the concern that the economy was fast approaching its limits, which had not been recognized prior to the NIPA revisions.

[24]A significant difficulty was that by the end of 1965, Federal Reserve staff, in line with best accepted practices of the day, started relying more heavily on a Phillips curve framework for forecasting inflation, which translated misestimates of economic activity gaps into biased forecasts of inflation. The difficulty is that the analysis failed to take into account that, in real time, gap-based forecasts of inflation are largely uninformative and often misleading (Orphanides and van Norden, 2003). As would be expected, the bias in output gap estimates during the 1960s and 1970s, resulted in inflation forecasts that were too optimistic (Orphanides, 2002, 2003). Private forecasts were no more accurate (Romer and Romer, 2000).

it is very clear that a tightening was long overdue, the Committee was split on whether action was needed. Examine the following from the go-around of comments and views on economic conditions and monetary policy from the *Minutes* for the November 23, 1965, FOMC meeting:

> [T]he gap between between actual and potential levels of activity will probably narrow further; and this should mean continued pressure on industrial capacity and the labor market. (Hayes statement, p. 33)
>
> Mr Mitchell did not see a threat to stability in the present and prospective rates of resource utilization (p. 59)
>
> The present situation was dangerous and worrisome because the economy was balanced at a high level of employment and output, but it was a very satisfactory level and one that he hoped could be maintained. (Maisel remarks, p. 67)
>
> Although the upcreep in prices had slowed and capacity limitations still did not appear to block further gains on output, many forecasts now emerging suggested a growth rate that could move the economy very close to full employment levels as 1966 unfolded. (Bopp remarks, p. 71)

Once again, assessments of the gap had the wrong sign. Once again, members of the Committee who were examining the policy problem in terms of gaps were misled. Policy was tightened after this meeting but the tightening had come too late.[25]

For 1978 the record suggests that the perceptions of Federal Reserve policymakers were even further removed from reality than in the two previous episodes. Once again, the economy was substantially overheated, and yet policy actions appeared to be based on the erroneous belief that a (negative) output gap was still lingering from the 1975 recession. The record suggests that the Committee recognized that the growth of the economy exceeded the growth of potential supply (as is confirmed with both the retrospective and real-time data in the middle panel of Figure 3). However, even in 1979 the Committee believed that a gap persisted. This is most clearly reflected in the February 20, 1979, Humphrey-Hawkins Report to Congress: "The narrowing of the gap between actual and potential output implies that a tighter hold on the nation's aggregate demand for goods and services is necessary if

---

[25]This tightening was the controversial increase in the discount rate on December 6, 1965, adopted at the urging of Chairman Martin. It should be noted that the Chairman himself was not favoring the gap-based policy analysis that was increasingly becoming more accepted at the time. The record suggests that on this occasion he would have favored tightening policy earlier, based on the observation that the rate of growth of the economy was unsustainably high, as is confirmed by both the real-time and retrospective readings in the middle panel of Figure 3.

inflationary forces are to be contained." Though the potential inflationary threat of pushing the economy beyond its limits were clearly understood, policymakers had the wrong sign on the gap during that time.[26]

The overview provided by Figure 4 suggests that the real-time prescriptions of the classic Taylor rule, with the implicit inflation target of 2 percent, appear to successfully capture the broad contours of actual policy over many years. The success appears closest during the period from the mid 1960s to the late 1970s—the Great Inflation. Since policy appears so similar to the classic rule over this period, a straightforward conclusion is that the experience of the Great Inflation would not have been prevented if this rule had been followed exactly. Importantly, the rather close match of the real-time prescriptions from the rule with actual policy during the Great Inflation is not evident in a comparison of policy with prescriptions based on current data, which serves to illustrate the potential pitfalls of historical policy analysis based on information which was not available when policy was made.[27] By contrast, the biggest and most systematic departures appear in the years prior to the Great Inflation and during the Volcker disinflation period.

Another way to examine the source of this difference is by comparing the real-time and ex post renditions of the output gap with the implicit output gap that would be necessary if the Taylor rule prescription were exactly matched over history by the actual federal funds rate. The top panel of Figure 5 presents such a comparison for the period since 1961. For the gap implied by the rule, the figure presents a 9-quarter moving average that smooths out high-frequency variations. As can be seen, the gap implied by the rule was extremely low during most of the 1970s, much like the actual real-time gap estimates. By contrast, policy during most of the 1980s and from 1994 to 1999 would have been consistent with the real-time Taylor rule only if the actual output gap were far greater than it actually was.

Two elements are important to understand the timing, magnitude and direction of the apparent errors in the real-time output gap estimates. First, the evolution of beliefs regarding estimates of the rate of unemployment that were consistent with full employment—what

---

[26]It is of interest to note that this significant error occured after estimates of potential output had been drastically scaled down. See Orphanides (2003c) for further details on the timing and size of those revisions.

[27]Indeed, the counterfactual simulations presented in Orphanides (2003c) indicate that application of the classic Taylor rule could not have averted the Great Inflation if policy were based on information actually available when decisions were made but better outcomes would have resulted if the rule could have been applied with information available ex post.

19

later became known as the natural rate or unemployment, NIRU or NAIRU and so forth. As is well known, estimates held with some confidence from the late 1940s to the early 1970s—around 4 percent—later proved to have been exceedingly optimistic. Economists, however, generally failed to recognize this change sufficiently quickly.[28] Okun's law may be used to illustrate the quantitative significance of misperceptions regarding the natural rate of unemployment for output gap errors. With an Okun's law coefficient of 2 (at the low end of the range of current parameterizations) a misperception of 2 percentage points on the unemployment gap translates to a 4 percentage point error in the measurement of the output gap. With Okun's original 3.3 coefficient, (which is more typical for the 1960s and early 1970s,) the error exceeds 6 percentage points.

The other key element for the huge misestimates of the output gap during the 1970s and even later was the productivity slowdown which had started in the late 1960s, worsened in the mid 1970s and persisted well into the 1990s, and still lacks a compelling explanation. Errors in estimates of output gaps due to such hard-to-explain changes in the growth rate of potential output can be particularly problematic as it is impossible to assess with any confidence the likely persistence of what may appear to be a once-in-a-lifetime event. To illustrate just how persistent such errors tend to be, the bottom panel of Figure 5 contrasts the historical output gap series from three years: 1973, 1982 and 1994. Although by 1982 about 15 years had passed from the suspected start of the slowdown, output gap estimates for the late 1960s and early 1970s still did not reflect nearly as much of the extent of the revision that was to be added to these estimates from that time until 1994. Indeed, the historical path of potential output was generally revised in one direction—downwards—for a period that lasted about twenty years. From the mid-1990s on, the reverse pattern started to appear in the data, although the recent revisions in the upward direction (as reflected in the CBO estimates) appeared to be faster than the revisions to the productivity slowdown a generation earlier. An optimistic interpretation of this behavior is that, conceivably, the recognition of the errors of the past may have led practitioners to dampen real-time estimates of output gaps towards zero, which in turn would reduce the magnitude of the

---

[28]Chairman Burns described this failure shortly after he left the Federal Reserve: "a broad consensus developed that an unemployment rate of about 4 percent corresponded to a practical condition of full employment ... now widely believed to be about 5 1/2 or 6 percent. ... But governmental policymakers ... were slow to recognize the changing meaning of unemployment statistics ... The Federal Reserve did not escape this lag of recognition." (Burns, 1979, p. 17).

errors associated with changes in the trend.[29] If history is a guide, on the other hand, it might take another decade or more before we can begin to evaluate the accuracy of estimates for the late 1990s.

The magnitude of the error apparent in historical estimates of the output gap from 1982, confirms that had the gap-based policies which appear to describe the Great Inflation period been continued during the early 1980s, the Great Inflation problem could have persisted. Indeed, the counterfactual simulations presented in Orphanides (2003c) using these data and an estimated model of the U.S. economy, confirm that had policy followed the classic Taylor rule, not only inflation would have followed a path very similar to that experienced during the Great Inflation, it would have remained at those high levels during the 1980s as well.

3.3   Forecast-Based Variants of the Classic Rule

The top panel of Figure 6 presents an illustration of two *forecast*-based variants of the classic rule. As already pointed out, given the emphasis that Federal Reserve policymakers have attached on forecasts over the past decades, it would be reasonable to expect that such rules could provide better descriptions of historical policy. The figure presents two such alternatives. The first replaces inflation with its forecast in the rule, but retains the most recent outcome for the gap. The second also replaces the output gap outcome with its forecast. (These rules are similar to the estimated Taylor-style rules in Clarida, Gali and Gertler (1999, 2000), and Orphanides (2001, 2002, 2003).)

For the illustration in the figure, I relied on forecasts of inflation over a four-quarter period starting from the quarter of latest available actual data. Given the one-quarter-lag in output data releases this implies, for each quarter t, a "year-ahead" forecast over the horizon $t-1$ to $t+3$. Similarly, for the rule that employs a forecast of the output gap I rely on the forecast for quarter $t+3$, a "year-ahead" from the latest actual output data for $t-1$. Forecasts at this horizon have been prepared by the Federal Reserve staff systematically as part of the Greenbook since 1969. (A few missing quarters in the early part of the sample reflect occasions when only shorter-horizon forecasts were produced by the staff. Shorter-

---

[29]In the limit, a robust approach is to "estimate" that the gap equals zero in every period, as a first approximation. This is equivalent to the robust approach of ignoring the output gap for policy analysis, as a first approximation. (Orphanides 2003b.)

horizon forecasts are available since 1966.) Starting from the quarterly dataset of these forecasts in Orphanides (2003), I extended the sample with the latest available Greenbook forecasts, to the end of 1997. The implied prescriptions from this rule, based on these forecasts, are shown in the figure for the 1969 to 1997 period. The end of this period is marked in the figure with the vertical solid line. As a hypothetical illustration of what such a policy rule might have suggested over the past five years, from 1998:1 to the current quarter (2002:4), I extended the figure by using, instead of the Greenbook forecasts, the forecasts available from the Survey of Professional Forecasters (SPF), (and for the output gap, the real-time CBO estimates of potential output).[30],[31]

Broadly, the contours of these forecast-based variants of the classic rule appear similar to the outcome-based variant presented in Figure 4. Less noticeable differences are also of interest, however. The contours of policy during the 1970s, in particular the timing of policy reversals, appears to be better captured with the forecast-based, rather than the outcome-based rule. The forecast based rules also do a somewhat better job of capturing the policy turning point of 1994. Evidently, an element of the preemptive strike against inflation that year is captured in these forecast-based variants, but not in the outcome-based version.

3.4 The Natural Growth Targeting Variation

Next, I provide a comparison of the classic rule with its money-growth-motivated variation, natural growth targeting. As an illustration of a *forecast*-based application of this alternative, I computed the settings implied by rule (10), maintaining, for direct comparability, Taylor's assumptions of an inflation target, $\pi^* = 2$ and, also a responsiveness coefficient, $\theta = \frac{1}{2}$.

$$\Delta i = \frac{1}{2}(\pi - 2) + \frac{1}{2}(\Delta q - \Delta q^*) \tag{13}$$

For this illustration, I relied on forecasts of inflation and real growth relative to the growth of potential supply over a four-quarter period starting from the quarter of latest available

---

[30] The SPF survey, a continuation of the quarterly NBER-ASA survey, is currently maintained by the Federal Reserve Bank of Philadelphia. Zarnowitz and Braun (1993), and Croushore (1993) provide informative descriptions.

[31] Parallel to the remark in footnote 16 regarding prescriptions based on CBO estimates, without knowing whether and how closely the SPF forecasts match the parallel Federal Reserve staff forecasts, rule prescriptions based on the CBO estimates and SPF forecasts should not be interpreted as necessarily bearing a resemblance to rule prescriptions that could have presumably been produced at the Federal Reserve in real time.

actual data. The source and timing of the data and forecasts is exactly as described for the forecast-based variants of the classic rule.

The bottom panel of Figure 6 presents this natural growth variant together with the classic version of the rule (reproduced from Figure 4). As can be seen from the figure, this variation of the Taylor framework appears more successful in capturing the actual setting of the federal funds rate over the past twenty years than the classic rendition. But on average, and consistently over many years, this policy would have suggested somewhat tighter policy settings than actual decisions. Evidently, this policy rule, consistent with a monetary targeting growth rule in the spirit of Friedman, would have consistently prescribed that faster progress towards disinflation should have been made during the 1970s and 1980s, as long as inflation deviated from its 2 percent target. But since the early 1990s, when inflation has hovered around this target, this policy rule appears to describe actual policy remarkably well and significantly better than the classic Taylor rule.

3.5 Estimated Policy Rules

Real-time data and forecasts may be used to estimate the implied policy rules reflected in the policy choices over the past several decades. For estimation, I consider a simple policy rule form that nests various variants of the Taylor rule, including the ones just discussed, as special cases:

$$i_t = \theta_0 + \theta_i i_{t-1} + \theta_\pi \pi_{t+3}^a + \theta_{\Delta y} \Delta^a y_{t+3} + \theta_y y_{t-1} \tag{14}$$

Here, $\pi_{t+3}^a = p_{t+3} - p_{t-1}$ is the "year-ahead" inflation forecast starting at $t-1$, as described earlier, $y_{t-1} = q_{t-1} - q_{t-1}^*$ is the output gap in period $t-1$, and $\Delta^a y_{t+3} = y_{t+3} - y_{t-1} = \Delta^a q_{t+3} - \Delta^a q_{t+3}^*$ is the "year-ahead" growth forecast relative to potential. Variables dated t and later reflect real-time forecasts formed during quarter t.

To nest the various alternatives, this specification is somewhat more general than the one estimated by Clarida, Gali and Gertler (1999, 2000), Orphanides (2001, 2003), and others, in that it includes a growth rate term with a horizon matching that of the horizon of the inflation forecast. Similar policy rules that also allow for such growth terms have been shown to offer simple characterizations of recent historical monetary policy in earlier studies (Orphanides and Wieland 1998, McCallum and Nelson 1999, Levin et al. 1999, 2002). These studies, however, relied on ex post revised data for estimation. Here I rely on real-time renditions.

In equation (14), the special case $\theta_i = \theta_{\Delta y} = 0$ corresponds to the inflation forecast version of the classic rule, and the case $\theta_i = 0$ and $\theta_{\Delta y} = -\theta_y > 0$ corresponds to the classic rule that targets the forecasts of both inflation and the output gap. The case $\theta_i = 1$, $\theta_y = 0$ and $\theta_{\Delta y} > 0$ corresponds to the natural growth variant.

Table 1 presents estimates of equation (14) for three different samples and two alternative sets of forecasts. The top panel presents estimates based on Greenbook forecasts, available through the end of 1997. The bottom panel shows corresponding estimates using the SPF survey which extends to the end of 2002. In both cases, the beginning of the sample is 1969. I report estimates for the full sample of available data as well two subsamples, one with data prior to the 1979:3 and another beginning in 1982:3.

The estimated equations indicate that this generalized version of the specific rules examined before broadly describes the time path of policy decisions with a rather surprising degree of consistency. Elements of both the classic variant of the rule and the natural growth variant appear in the estimates. The restrictions implied by both the classic and natural growth special cases are rejected by the data. There is a substantial element of inertia, but θ_i is smaller that one. And the responses to both the output gap and to output growth are positive.

During both subsamples, policy appeared to respond strongly to inflation forecasts.[32] This contrasts sharply with findings (based on ex post data analysis) suggesting that Federal Reserve policymakers responded to inflation insufficiently strongly for economic stability during the Great Inflation. (Clarida, Gali and Gertler (1999, 2000).) Rather the estimation over the two subsamples identifies another important but subtle difference: it suggests that policy responded relatively more heavily to the level of the output gap rather than the growth rate of output during the Great Inflation and has responded much less to the output gap relative to inflation since then. As argued in Orphanides (2003, 2003b), although subtle, a change of this nature likely contributed importantly to the apparent improvement in macroeconomic stability over the past two decades, relative to the earlier period.[33]

---

[32]These estimated rules satisfy the stability criteria detailed in Woodford (2002).

[33]See also McCallum (2001), Gaspar and Smets (2002), Mishkin (2002), and Orphanides and Williams (2003), for related arguments indicating how excessive emphasis on output gaps can prove counterproductive for economic stability.

In summary, based on these estimates, somewhat different variants of the Taylor rule appear to capture historical behavior during and after the Great Inflation, but the differences are subtler than they appear on the basis of retrospective analysis. In particular, the policies pursued during the Great Inflation do not appear to be obviously flawed or to be out of line with broad characterizations of good policy practice based on the Taylor-rule framework.

4 The Genesis of Activist Stabilization Policy at the Federal Reserve

Thus far we have seen that starting with the Accord, Federal Reserve policy can be broadly characterized with the Taylor-rule framework with considerable consistency. In this section, I delve further back in an attempt to identify when this approach begins to offer a useful characterization of the monetary policy debate, and to track the resulting policies and economic outcomes from the viewpoint of this framework. The evidence leads us to the 1920s, a period which marked, in effect, the birth of modern central banking in the United States. Remarkably, the 1920s span both what Friedman and Schwartz termed "the high tide of the reserve system," as well as the origins of the System's greatest failure—the Great Depression.

My aim in this section is to briefly review some basic aspects of the state of knowledge in empirical macroeconomics during the 1920s and relate the salient characteristics of policy to the Taylor-rule framework. A number of issues, of course, are left untouched. For completeness, I refer the reader to the comprehensive treatments of the period provided by Friedman and Schwartz (1963) and Meltzer (2003).

An underlying premise in my description is that the objectives of the Federal Reserve System during that period were interpreted, from a modern perspective, as a mandate for general economic stability and welfare, which in turn implied that, to the extent possible, the Federal Reserve would want to pursue countercyclical monetary policy, or, which is the same in modern parlance, reduce fluctuations in the "output gap."[34] Indeed, as noted by

---

[34]To be sure, these objectives should be seen in the context of the gold standard, which, at times, constrained policy options directed towards the domestic economy. However, because the United States enjoyed a relatively large quantity of gold reserves, it was believed that the Federal Reserve had some flexibility for pursuing objectives beyond the maintenance of the standard. For example, as Burgess explained in November 1929, whereas "bank of issue policy in other countries, both at other times and even more recently has been largely determined by the position of the gold standard," because of its reserve cushion, "[Federal Reserve] policy can be determined not by what it has to do, but by what is best for it to do for the well-being

Burgess (1936) (an influential economist at the Federal Reserve Bank of New York during this period), although section 14 of the original Federal Reserve Act stated that rates of discount "shall be fixed with a view of accommodating commerce and business," this could not have been and was not interpreted literally. Rather, he explained: "The only reasonable interpretation of the phrase is that policy is to be directed towards the general economic welfare of the country." (Burgess, 1936, p. 296.) On the other hand, price stability, per se, was not considered a primary objective. However, it was implicitly understood that if policy were successful in stabilizing business, prices would generally also remain stable. In addition, the gold standard provided a nominal anchor.

Though the Federal Reserve started its operations in 1914, it was not until 1920-21 that the System finally had the opportunity to start formulating the nation's monetary policy in earnest. Earlier, and in particular during the turbulence immediately following the end of World War I, policy appeared subordinated to supporting Treasury financing operations. As early as 1921 the basic principles that underlay monetary policy during the decade begun to appear and by 1922/23 all pieces fell in place and the modern era had begun.

The timing of a number of developments contributed to the genesis of modern policy. First, the abrupt rise and fall in prices and economic activity experienced in 1919-1920 (shown in Figure 7) provided an impetus to investigate how monetary policy could assert its authority and assume an active role for improving economic stability. Second, the Federal Reserve started to understand the role of and recognize the power of open market operations as a policy instrument. Third, for the first time since its beginnings, the System could rely on solid macroeconomic statistics for formulating policy, the result of an intense effort to that effect over the previous years. Starting with March 1922, the Federal Reserve began publication of aggregate indexes of trade and production in its monthly Bulletin and from that point on, analyses of the movements in aggregate prices, production and credit data became a regular aspect of policy analysis at the Board.[35] Finally, advances in statistical

_____

of the country." (Burgess, 1930, p. 509). (It is interesting to note the timing of these remarks, in light of the subsequent events and Federal Reserve policy actions.)

[35] The Board's early data collection effort was concentrated in New York City in the Division of Analysis and Research under the direction of Parker Willis. In May 1922 the Division was transferred to Washington D.C. (*Ninth Annual Report for 1922*, p. 39) and in July 1923 it was merged with the Office of the Statistician, creating the Division of Research and Statistics with Walter Stewart as Director (*Tenth Annual Report for 1923*, p. 62-63). Yohe (1990) provides a history of the early years of the development of this Division. A separate statistical analysis group at the FRB of New York, headed by Carl Snyder, also contributed importantly to the availability of aggregate statistics.

modeling, coupled with the available aggregate data, allowed economists and policymakers to start thinking about the monetary policy problem in terms of the interrelationships of prices, production, employment, and credit, as well as the influence of monetary policy decisions on these variables. Especially important were advances in index theory and filtering both for seasonal and secular trend effects which allowed the measurement and systematic study of business cycle phenomena.[36] And with these developments in place, versions of statistical relationships of such common modern-era concepts as the "Phillips curve" and "Okun's law" were quickly developed.

The importance of measurement for policy *control* was understood very early. Shortly before joining the Board staff, Walter Stewart introduced a study on industrial production indexes that he presented at the December 1920 annual meeting of the American Economic Association by noting that: "The fluctuations in the physical volume of production must be measured before they can be interpreted or controlled." (1921, p. 57), After presenting measures of the magnitude of output lost during earlier recessions—which in his view reflected wasted output—Stewart argued in favor of stabilization policies using language we often associate with 1930s era, post-*General-Theory* Keynesian doctrine. He concluded that: "To regard waste of such magnitude as the necessary accompaniment of business cycles and to give up the problem of stabilizing the level of production is to confess our incompetence" (p. 1921).[37]

On the analytical front, the beginning of the decade saw a flurry of activity and proposals for effective monetary policy. In another paper presented at the same December 1920 meeting, Sprague (1921) put forth a proposal to "base the discount rate largely on the observed effects of credit expansion," with the aim of "lessening price fluctuations within particular business cycles, checking somewhat the upward movement, and thereby lessening the subsequent decline ... [that is] administer the reserve system in such a way as to moderate the fluctuations of the business cycle" (p. 28). In essence, Sprague was proposing a simple Taylor rule for the Federal Reserve, raising the discount rate in periods of inflation,

---

[36] An important example of these developments can be found in the inaugural issue of the *Review of Economic Statistics* (January 1919) which was dedicated to the measurement of the business cycle and detailed methods for data detrending and seasonal adjustment, allowing the identification of the cyclical component of time series.

[37] It is of interest to note, in this context, that many elements of the activist *fiscal* policy discussion of the 1930s, which became elements of the activist *monetary* policy discussion more recently, bear important similarities to the activist *monetary* policy discussion during the 1920s.

and reducing it in periods of deflation. Not unexpectedly, the proposal was met with strong opposition, as evidenced by the discussion at the meeting (Leffingwell, 1921). Fortunately, for the purpose of historical analysis, elements of that debate appeared in print. Adolph Miller, who had been a member of the Federal Reserve Board since its beginning, (and who was, at the time, the only economist on the Board), published a detailed view of the Board's position on this matter. As he articulated it, not only would Sprague's rule be inconsistent with the mandate of the System, but a more ambitious framework for policy could achieve better economic performance also. According to Miller, a large number of factors influenced the determination of appropriate discount policy, not just past price movements. Perhaps most importantly, he stressed that monetary policy needed to be preemptive, anticipating positions such as those reflected decades later in the comments cited in section 2:

> Prevention, rather than control, should be the objective of a competent credit policy in the United States ... [Credit policy] aims to deal with tendencies or situations in the making, rather than to await their development before acting. While credit policy uses the rate as an instrument, it does not make the rate its only reliance, and when it uses the rate, uses it in time so as to prevent the necessity of resort to extreme and punitive levels. (p.193)

Anticipating future debates, Miller went on to suggest that, in principle, the Federal Reserve could pursue preemptive policies along the lines of inflation targeting: "As a theoretical proposition, therefore, it is entirely conceivable that the discount policy of the federal reserve system might be governed by indications of impending price changes, with a view of mitigating their cyclical fluctuations," (p. 193), but insisted that policy, instead, should always be taking into account "a great variety of factors," including "the state of business, and trade ... the state of money markets ... accidental economic disturbances, sometimes political conditions and the international situation, the stage of the business cycle, price movements and the state of banking reserves" (p. 195). In essence, Miller, offered an early parallel to the more recent debates regarding the robust guidance of a simple rule—as suggested by Sprague—against the promise of superior outcomes from pursuing the "optimal" policy of the moment.

But on what basis could such a preemptive policy be formulated by the Federal Reserve? The answer to that was to be provided at the turn of 1923, when the Federal Reserve, for the first time, undertook what in today's parlance would be called a "pre-emptive strike against inflation."

By the end of 1922, the volume of production and employment were advancing briskly and the Federal Reserve was concerned that the economy was becoming overheated. Although actual prices did not indicate that inflation was underway, production had exceeded what was perceived to be its "normal" level, that is a positive "output gap" appeared on the horizon, using today's language.[38]

Policy was tightened in March 1923. A detailed rationale was published in the March Bulletin. The most important observation was the identification of a level of activity corresponding to the full utilization of productive resources—in essence what we now call "potential output:"

> When, however, production reaches the limits imposed by the available supplies of labor, plant capacity, and transportation facilities—in fact, whenever the productive energies and resources of the country are employed at full capacity—output can not be enlarged by an increased use of credit and by further increases in prices. (p. 283)

The key idea was to target economic activity at its potential as an operational policy guide. As Miller explained during the 1926 Stabilization Hearings, referring to this passage from 1923:

> This passage not only points to a situation and shows how it was interpreted, ..., it indicates that an attitude of mind had begun to crystallize in the Federal reserve system that practically constitutes it an incipient guiding principle for the system. (United States Congress, 1927, p. 709.)

---

[38] As noted earlier, advances in filtering and the availability of data resulted in measures of such "gaps" whose adoption quickly became standard practice. The concepts of "natural growth," "secular trend" and "normal" (that is detrended and seasonally adjusted) became common in analyses of production and sales data. Snyder (1923) and Burgess (1924) offer early illustrations of the use of these concepts by System economists (and, in Snyder's case, statisticians.) Snyder presents one of the earliest illustrations of such employment and output "gaps" and an early version of Okun's law. As one would expect, virtually simultaneously, researchers started examining the interrelationships of these "gaps" and price movements, providing early versions of "Phillips curves." An early such example can be found in Burgess. Interestingly, although it is by now widely known that as early as 1926 Irving Fisher had already described the statistical relationship between price inflation and *unemployment*, much less well known is that even earlier, in three studies he published between 1923 and 1925, he had already described the statistical relationship between price inflation and the *output gap* concept of his day, that is "the physical volume of trade (duly corrected for secular trend and seasonal variation)," (1923, p, 1026). Fisher concluded that "this one element, *rapidity in price movement*, during the period 1914-22 seems to account, almost completely, for the ups and downs of business," (1923 p. 1027, emphasis in the original). The correlation between prices and production or sales was widely noted but the direction of causality, a question examined by King (1924), was, and arguably remains, very much in dispute.

Arguably, this marked the beginning of the era of reliance on the level of real economic activity relative to "potential," that is current and forecasted "output" and "employment" gaps, for monetary control at the Federal Reserve.[39]

The *Tenth Annual Report for 1923*, articulated this policy framework further.[40] The report noted the presence of lags in the effect of monetary policy:

> The influence of the change of discount rates by the reserve banks can not be measured by any immediate effect that they might be expected to have on the total volume of borrowing at member banks. ... It requires, therefore, some time for a rate change to show its effects in the altered lending operations of the banks" (p. 4-5)

and reiterated the lagging nature of observed prices as an indicator, and the need for pre-emptive action to smooth the business cycle.

By most accounts, the resulting activist approach to policy articulated in 1923 and practiced in subsequent years proved remarkably successful, not only by the standards of the day but by today's standards as well. The period from 1923 to the end of 1929 was one of prosperity and stability—a *"new era"*.

Throughout this period, the basic rationale for policy action and framework for analysis remained fundamentally the same. In reviewing the policy framework at the time, Burgess (1927) observed:[41]

> A rate policy which, other things being equal, threw its influence towards firm money conditions when business was very active and towards easy money when business was in depression, might be expected to offer effective aid towards reducing the fluctuations of the business cycle. Thus a continuous study of the condition of general business in relation to the trends of normal growth indicated by the experience of past years becomes an important aid in determining rate policy. (Burgess 1927, p. 197-198)

---

[39]Miller also highlighted the key role of the data availability for the new activist policy regime. Referring to the same passage from the March 1923 *Bulletin* he observed: "Such a statement could not have been made by the Federal Reserve Board prior to the development of these various indexes and diagnostic devices, so to speak" (p. 283)

[40]Though critical of the proposed policy framework in the report, Friedman and Schwartz (1963) praise the report for presenting a "highly subtle and sophisticated" analysis of the problem of devising guides to credit policy and reflecting "an altogether different intellectual level" than earlier writings (p. 251). The key sections, in particular *Guides to Credit Policy*, were apparently written by Walter Stewart and Adolph Miller. (See also Yohe, 1990 and Meltzer 2003.)

[41]This quote follows a diagram presenting one of the output gap concepts of the day. The legend reads: "Diagram 32: The volume of trade compared to the trend of growth of past years."

At a presentation before the Academy of Political Science that year he also noted that: "the theory that it is part of our business to try to cut off the tops and the bottoms of some the business cycles" was "fairly generally accepted in the Federal Reserve System" and "has been generally acted upon ... perhaps most definitely exhibited in the open market operations," (Burgess 1927b, p. 143-144).

This same activist, preemptive policy framework was also in place during the 1928/29 period, leading into the stock market crash of October 1929 and the brink of the Great Depression. This preemption is of special interest because policy was deliberately tight before the crash, and, based on subsequent outcomes, particularly the onset of the Great Depression, the wisdom of this tight policy has been questioned and Federal Reserve policy during 1929 is sometimes characterized as deeply flawed. It is therefore of some importance to identify the underlying causes of this tight policy.

A major accusation is that policymakers actively tried to "pop" the developing stock market bubble, which was perceived as a threat to the continued progress and stability of the economy. Importantly, it is noted that prices were slightly falling during the tightening period, which could have provided an argument against it. Indeed, policymakers exhibited tremendous concern about the rising stock market and openly suggested their discomfort with the speculative frenzy on Wall Street. Policymakers loudly complained about a "diversion" of Federal Reserve credit towards this speculative activity and agonized over ways in which they could ensure that this credit flow could be stopped without negative side effects on the availability of credit for productive uses. This reasoning, it is sometimes argued, is what provided the rationale for the misguided pursuit of tight policies.

But was the tight policy of 1929 inconsistent with the successful "modern" framework that was in place earlier during the decade? While it may be the case that the bubble-popping reasoning appears flawed retrospectively, at least to most observers, this flaw does not necessarily imply that the tight money policy of 1929 was inconsistent with the pre-emptive activist approach that was deemed to be successful earlier in the decade. Neither does it imply that if policymakers had ignored the speculative frenzy in Wall Street and merely concentrated on the implications of this activity for general credit conditions and the outlook for inflation, policy would have been markedly different. Rather, economic developments prior to the crash suggest the opposite conclusion.

31

In particular, the tight money policy of 1928-1929 could be explained as a policy patterned after the happy experience of 1923, and merely reflected an attempt to control an overheated economy in order to improve the odds of the continuation of favorable overall conditions—that is, another "pre-emptive strike against inflation" using today's vocabulary. Indeed, by 1929, industrial production had exceeded its "normal" level, suggesting that the policy tightening would not have been inconsistent with an "output gap" based policy framework, as employed in 1923. The middle panel of Figure 7 presents the index of industrial production and a related detrended series (an output gap measure from the time) confirming this concern.[42] Further, not all price indexes at the time suggested deflation. The top panel of Figure 7 compares two relevant indexes, one for Wholesale Commodities Prices (WCP) and the General Price Index (GPI), which appeared to be the preferred measure of prices at the Federal Reserve Bank of New York at the time. As can be seen, while the WCP indicated some deflation, the GPI reflected steady inflation.[43] In addition, a policy that was preemptive in nature would be less concerned with the slight slide in actual *past* prices and more concerned about the outlook for the future, so even the slight decline in the WCP index should not have served to deter the tightening either.

This "modern" explanation for the tight policies of 1929 was, in fact, articulated at the time by Reed (1930):

> Taken in conjunction with the enlarged volume of trade and the rising tendencies in general prices, evidence of restricted credit growth goes far to deny the thesis that we must look principally to speculative rise of credit to find adequate explanation of the rising tendency of money rates in 1928 and 1929. (p. 174.)

> Threatened loss of credit control was the real source of apprehension, and speculative use of credit had to be checked, not because such credit was made unavailable for other uses, but because speculative demands threatened an excessive expansion of credit in general. (p. 176.)

---

[42] The output gap series shown, from the NBER historical database, appears to be based on 1931 data. Series from earlier years, for example, Diagram 32 in Burgess (1927, p. 197) (with data through he first half of 1927) and a figure prepared for the January 1928 OMIC meeting by the Federal Reserve Bank of New York (with data to the end of 1927) appear to be based on similar estimates of the underlying trend. The industrial production index shown is from the Board's *Annual Report for 1929*.

[43] Part of the difference, especially for 1929, is due to the fact that the GPI included, by construction, a 10% weight on the prices of securities, bonds, and stocks. While the wisdom of this practice may be retrospectively questioned (and even compared with that of recent suggestions to include equity prices in general price indexes for policy purposes), what matters for this analysis is that this practice was considered useful and was accepted as such at the time. Related to this aspect of the construction of the GPI during the 1920s is the influence of interest rates on measured CPI during the late 1970s and early 1980s.

Closer examination of the policy discussions at the time, as reflected in the available minutes of the Open Market Investment Committee (OMIC), and the memoranda prepared by the staff for those meetings, suggests that this explanation may have considerable merit. The policy record confirms that the Federal Reserve would have preferred that the advances in equity values during 1929 were checked prior to the crash, but does not present evidence of an attempt to "target" equity values per se. As was stated most clearly in a much quoted passage from the February 1929 Bulletin:

> The Federal Reserve Board neither assumes the right nor has it any disposition to set itself up as an arbiter of security speculation (p. 93).

In fact, the OMIC was well aware of the hazards of attempting to assess either the extent to which the market reflected a "bubble" or when a correction would take place. According to the "Preliminary Memorandum for the OMIC" for the November 14, 1928, meeting:

> As far as stock speculation is concerned, it is, of course, impossible to set a date when the present movement will culminate. It is impossible to pass judgment now upon the extent to which the recent movement is upon a sound economic basis and the extent to which it represents boom psychology. The question can only be settled by time and the test of high interest rates.

The difficulty, rather, was that the sharp rise in equity values, by facilitating stock issuance at favorable terms for corporations, created an environment of easy overall monetary conditions, despite the Federal Reserve's tight money policy. According to Reed (1930), funds raised by corporations issuing stock nearly doubled from 1927 to 1928 and then doubled again from 1928 to 1929 (p. 176). From this perspective, monetary conditions, in a sense broader than what is reflected in short-term interest rates, would have appeared too easy.

In addition, the OMIC closely followed business conditions throughout the year, cognizant of the fact that at least some sectors of the economy—if not business in general—could be negatively affected by the tight rate environment. But as late as September, at the last meeting of the OMIC before the crash, the outlook did not appear particularly alarming. The September 24, 1929 "Preliminary Memorandum for the OMIC" noted:

> Business is still operating at a high level, above any of the computed 'normal' lines based on previous experience and allowing for growth. In recent weeks, however, there has been a declining tendency in a number of basic industries. ...

These recessions have not, however, progressed far enough to warrant definite conclusions as to the trend.

In modern terms, the analysis as of September 24, 1929 suggested that output exceeded the econony's potential, that is the "output gap" was positive, which, on the basis of the preemptive "gap" based policy framework that appears to have been in place plainly required maintaining the tight policy stance that was in place.[44]

In summary, the 1920s, including the high-tide years as well as the tight policies leading to the disastrous crash and the beginning of the Great Depression appear to be consistent with the key aspects of Taylor's framework for interest-rate-based policy analysis. Retrospectively, the attempts at activist stabilization of the economy during the 1920s, using forecasts of economic activity and perceptions of "normal" levels of activity for guidance, appeared successful for a time, only to lead policymakers into a major policy error at the end of the decade. I note that this analysis does not include events *after* the crash and is therefore silent on the sources of the subsequent policy errors documented by Friedman and Schwartz (1963) and Meltzer (2003).

5 Conclusion

This paper provides a broad overview of monetary policy in the United States through the lens of a Taylor-rule framework for policy analysis. The framework proves useful for interpreting past policy decisions and mistakes. Policy during the 1920s, as well as since the Treasury-Federal Reserve Accord appears to have been broadly consistent with the Taylor-rule framework. Policy evolved somewhat over time, but when closely examined within the context of the information available and policymaker perceptions in real time, this change is subtler than usually appears at first glance with retrospective analysis.

The history reviewed covers eras of stability, including periods of great prosperity such as the 1920s and the 1960s. As we know, during both of these periods, hopes were raised,

---

[44]To be sure, this analysis does not preclude the straightforward justification for the 1928-1929 tightenings suggested by the optimal control approach to incorporating equity valuation in policy analysis, as in Cecchetti et al. (2002). The analysis here suggests that the more conventional gap-based preemptive strategy may provide an adequate explanation. (Cecchetti et al. point out that, in principle, a willingness to rely on "output gap" measures for policy decisions should carry over to equity valuation "misalignments," as neither can be accurately measured. Alternatively, of course, this could be seen as an argument for relying *neither* on estimates of the gap *nor* on equity valuation "misalignments.")

perhaps inevitably in light of human nature, that prosperity would continue unabated, and that business cycle fluctuations could, perhaps, be largely eliminated with greater refinement of policy actions. Subsequent events were not kind to such hopes. The policy framework in place during these two periods did not avert the subsequent chain of events that led, respectively, to the brink of the Great Depression and the Great Inflation. Evidently, with its relatively blunt instruments, monetary policy does not lend itself to great refinement.

On its face, adoption of a Taylor-rule framework as a guide to policy would appear to describe behavior that would be systematic and prudent in practice. And yet history seems to suggest that this is not sufficient to ensure that monetary policy will stay a steady course. The variants of the framework that best describe policy during the 1920s and 1960s, in particular, require accurate assessments of the evolution of trends in the economy and identification of what is the "normal" or "potential" level of economic activity. But policymakers, no matter how good their intentions may be, have only limited information to form the necessary judgments about such concepts. Such concepts, therefore, cannot necessarily provide a reliable guide for steady monetary policy. Over history, efforts at activist control of the economy have been successful at times, but have also led to spectacular failures. Reduced overall activism has been consistent with better outcomes since the Great Inflation, but it is arguably too early to evaluate the recent experiences in great detail. In the end, given the historical experience and our state of knowledge, identification of the best monetary policy practice remains uncertain.

References

Batini, N., Haldane A., 1999. Forward-looking Rules for Monetary Policy. In Taylor, 1999.

Batini, N., Nelson, E., 2000. Optimal Horizons for Inflation Targeting. Bank of England Working Paper 119, July.

Bernanke, B.S., Mishkin, F.S., 1997. Inflation Targeting: A New Framework for Monetary Policy? *Journal of Economic Perspectives*, 11(2), 97-116.

Bernanke, B.S., Laubach, T., Mishkin, F.S., Posen, A., 1998. *Inflation Targeting: Lessons from the International Experience*. Princeton University Press, Princeton.

Burgess, W.R., 1924. Fluctuations in Retail and Wholesale Trade. In Persons et al., 1924.

Burgess, W.R., 1927. *The Reserve Banks and the Money Market. Harper and Brothers, New York.*

Burgess, W.R., 1927b. What the Federal Reserve System is Doing to Promote Business Activity. In *Stabilizing Business*, Proceedings of the Academy of Political Science, April 8, 1927 Meeting, Columbia University, New York, 1927.

Burgess, W.R., 1930. Guide to Bank of Issue Policy. *Proceedings of the Academy of Political Science*, 13(4), 508-513, January.

Burgess, W.R., 1936. *The Reserve Banks and the Money Market*. Second Edition, Harper and Brothers, New York.

Burns, A., 1979. *The Anguish of Central Banking*. The 1979 Per Jacobson Lecture, Belgrade, Yugoslavia, September 30.

Brunner, K., Meltzer, A.H., 1993. *Money and the Economy: Issues in Monetary Analysis*. The Rafaelle Mattioli Lectures, University of Cambridge, Cambridge.

Bryant, R.C., Hooper, P., Mann, C. (Eds), 1993. *Evaluating Policy Regimes: New Research in Empirical Macroeconomics*, Brookings, Washington DC.

Cecchetti, S., Genberg, H., Wadhwani, S., 2002. Asset Prices in a Flexible Inflation Targeting Framework. NBER working paper 8970, June.

Christiano, L.J., Fitzgerald T.J., 2001. The Band Pass Filter. Mimeo, July.

Clarida, R., Gali, J., Gertler, M., 1999. The Science of Monetary Policy. *Journal of Economic Literature*, 37(4), 1661-1707, December.

Clarida, R., Gali, J., Gertler, M., 2000. Monetary Policy Rules and Macroeconomic Stability: Evidence and Some Theory. *Quarterly Journal of Economics*, 115 (1), 147-180, February.

Cooper, J.P., Fischer, S., 1972. Simulations of Monetary Rules in the FRB-MIT-Penn Model. *Journal of Money, Credit and Banking* 4(2), 384-396, May.

Cooper, J.P., Fischer, S., 1974. Monetary and Fiscal Policy in the Fully Stochastic St. Louis Econometric Model. *Journal of Money, Credit and Banking* 6(1), 1-22, February.

Congressional Budget Office, 2002. *The Budget and Economic Outlook*. United States Congress, Washington DC.

Council of Economic Advisers, 1990. Economic Report of the President. United States Government Printing Office, Washington DC.

Croushore, D., 1993. Introducing: The Survey of Professional Forecasters. Federal Reserve Bank of Philadelphia *Business Review*, November/December, 3-13.

Federal Open Market Committee, 2000. Modifications to the FOMC's Disclosure Procedures. January 19.

Fischer, S., Cooper, J.P., 1973. Stabilization Policy and Lags. *Journal of Political Economy*, 81(4), 847-877, July-August.

Fisher, I., 1923. The Business Cycle Largely a 'Dance of the Dollar.' *Journal of the American Statistical Association*, 18(144), 1024-1028, December.

Fisher, I., 1924. Fluctuations in Price-Levels. In Persons et al. (1924).

Fisher, I., 1926. A Statistical Relation between Unemployment and Price Changes. *International Labor Review*, 13(6), 785-92, June 1926. (Reprinted in *Journal of Political Economy*, 81(2, Part 1) 496-502, March-April 1973.)

Friedman, M. 1968. The Role of Monetary Policy. *American Economic Association Papers and Proceedings*, 58(1), March, 1-17.

Friedman, M., Schwartz, A.J., 1963. *A Monetary History of the United States: 1867–1960.* Princeton University Press, Princeton NJ.

Gaspar, V., Smets, F., 2002. Monetary Policy, Price Stability and Output Gap Stabilization *International Finance* 5(2), 193-211, Summer.

Goldenweiser, E., Hagen, E.E., 1944. Jobs After the War. *Federal Reserve Bulletin*, 30(5), May 1944.

Goodfriend, M., 1991. Interest Rates and the Conduct of Monetary Policy. Carnegie-Rochester Conference Series, 34, 7–30.

Greenspan, A., 1997. *Rules vs. discretionary monetary policy,* Remarks at the 15th Anniversary Conference of the Center for Economic Policy Research at Stanford University, Stanford, California, September 5.

Greenspan, A., 1999. The Federal Reserve's semiannual report on monetary policy, Testimony before the Committee on Banking and Financial Services, U.S. House of Representatives July 22.

Greenspan, A., 2000. Technology and the economy. Remarks Technology and the economy Before the Economic Club of New York, New York, New York January 13.

Heller, W., Gordon, K., Tobin, J., 1961. The American Economy in 1961: Problems and Policies. In *January 1961 Economic Report of the President and the Economic Situation and Outlook*, Hearings before the Joint Economic Committee, Congress of the United States, U.S. Government Printing Office, Washington, D.C.

Henderson, D., McKibbin, W.J., 1993. A Comparison of Some Basic Monetary Policy Regimes for Open Economies: Implications of Different Degrees of Instrument Adjustment and Wage Persistence. Carnegie-Rochester Conference Series on Public Policy 39, 221-318.

Hetzel, R.L., Leach, R.F., 2001. The Treasury-Fed Accord: A New Narrative Account. *Federal Reserve Bank of Richmond, Economic Quarterly*, 87(1), 33-55, Winter.

Horwich, G. (Ed.), 1967. *Monetary Process and Policy: A Symposium.* Irwin, Homewood, Illinois.

Joint Committee on the Economic Report, 1949. *Monetary, Credit, and Fiscal Policies.* United States Printing Office, Washington DC.

King, W.I., 1924. Trade Cycles and Factory Production. In Persons et al. (1924).

Kuroda, I. (Ed.), 1997. *Towards More Effective Monetary Policy.* St Martin's Press, New York.

Laubach, T., 2001. Measuring the NAIRU: Evidence from Seven Economies. *Review of Economics and Statistics*, 83(2), May, 218–231.

Laubach, T., Williams, J.C., 2001. Measuring the Natural Rate of Interest. Finance and Economics Discussion Series 2001-56, Federal Reserve Board, November.

Leffingwell, R. C., 1921. The Discount Policy of the Federal Reserve Banks: Discussion. *American Economic Review*, 11(1), 30-36, March.

Leitemo, K., Lonning, I., 2002. Monetary Policymaking without the Output Gap. Norges Bank, March.

Levin, A., Wieland, V., Williams, J.C., 1999. Robustness of Simple Monetary Policy Rules under Model Uncertainty. In Taylor, 1999.

Levin, A., Wieland, V., Williams, J.C., 2003. The Performance of Forecast-based Monetary Policy Rules under Model Uncertainty. *American Economic Review*, forthcoming.

Martin, W. M., 1965. Remarks before the 59th annual meeting of the Life Insurance Association of America, New York City, December 8.

McCallum, B.T., 1988. Robustness Properties of a Rule for Monetary Policy. Carnegie-Rochester Conference Series on Public Policy, vol. 29, Autumn, 173-203.

McCallum, B.T., 1990. Could a Monetary Base Rule Have Prevented the Great Depression? *Journal of Monetary Economics*, 26, 3-26.

McCallum, B.T., 1993. Discretion versus Policy Rules in Practice, Two Critical Points: A Comment. Carnegie-Rochester Conference Series on Public Policy, 39, December, 215-220.

McCallum, B.T., 2000. Alternative Monetary Policy Rules: A Comparison with Historical Settings for the United States, the United Kingdom, and Japan. *FRB Richmond Economic Quarterly*, 86(1), 49-79, Winter.

McCallum, B.T., 2001. Should Monetary Policy Respond Strongly to Output Gaps? *American Economic Review*, 91(2), 258-262, May.

McCallum, B.T., Nelson, E., 1999. Performance of Operational Policy Rules in an Estimated Semiclassical Structural Model. In Taylor, 1999.

Meltzer, A.H., 1987. Limits of Short-Run Stabilization Policy. Economic Inquiry, 25, 1-14.

Meltzer, A.H., 2003. *A History of the Federal Reserve: Volume I*, University of Chicago Press, Chicago.

Meyer, L.H., 2002. *Rules and Discretion*, Remarks At the Owen Graduate School of Management, Vanderbilt University, Nashville, Tennessee, January 16.

Miller, A.C., 1921. Federal Reserve Policy. *American Economic Review*, 11(2), 177-206, June.

Mishkin, F.S., 2002. The Role of Output Stabilization in the Conduct of Monetary Policy. NBER Working Paper, 9291, October.

Nessen, M., 1999. Targeting Inflation over the Short, Medium and Long Term. Working Paper, Sveriges Riksbank.

Okun, A., 1962. Potential Output: Its Measurement and Significance. In *American Statistical Association 1962 Proceedings of the Business and Economic Section*, Washington, D.C.: American Statistical Association.

Orphanides, A., 2000. Activist Stabilization Policy and Inflation: The Taylor Rule in the 1970s. Finance and Economics Discussion Series, 2000-13, Federal Reserve Board, February.

Orphanides, A., 2001. Monetary Policy Rules Based on Real-Time Data. *American Economic Review*, 91(4), 964-85, September.

Orphanides, A., 2002. Monetary Policy Rules and the Great Inflation. *American Economic Review*, 92(2), 115-120, May.

Orphanides, A., 2003. Monetary Policy Rules, Macroeconomic Stability and Inflation: A View from the Trenches. *Journal of Money, Credit and Banking*, forthcoming.

Orphanides, A., 2003b. Monetary Policy Evaluation With Noisy Information. *Journal of Monetary Economics*, 50(3), 605-631, April.

Orphanides, A., 2003c. The Quest for Prosperity Without Inflation. *Journal of Monetary Economics*, 50(3), 633-663, April.

Orphanides, A., 2003d. Monetary Policy in Deflation: The Liquidity Trap in History and Practice. Working Paper, April.

Orphanides, A., Porter, R., Reifschneider, D., Tetlow, R., Finan, F., 2000. Errors in the Measurement of the Output Gap and the Design of Monetary Policy. *Journal of Economics and Business*, 52(1/2), 117-141, January/April.

Orphanides, A., van Norden, S., 2002. The Unreliability of Output Gap Estimates in Real Time. *Review of Economics and Statistics*, 84(4), 569-583, November.

Orphanides, A., van Norden, S., 2003. The Reliability of Inflation Forecasts Based on Output Gap Estimates in Real Time. CIRANO Scientific Series 2003s-1, January 2003.

Orphanides, A., Wieland, V., 1998. Price Stability and Monetary Policy Effectiveness when Nominal Interest Rates are Bounded at Zero. Finance and Economics Discussion Series Working Paper 1998-35, Board of Governors of the Federal Reserve System.

Orphanides, A., Wieland, V., 2000. Efficient Monetary Policy Design Near Price Stability. *Journal of the Japanese and International Economies*, 14, 327-365.

Orphanides, A., Williams, J.C., 2002. Robust Monetary Policy Rules with Unknown Natural Rates *Brookings Papers on Economic Activity*, 2:2002, 63-145.

Orphanides, A., Williams, J.C., 2003. Imperfect Knowledge, Inflation Expectations and Monetary Policy. In Woodford, M. ed., *Inflation Targeting*, University of Chicago Press, Chicago, forthcoming.

Persons W.M., Foster, W.T., Hettinger, A.J. Jr., 1924. *The Problem of Business Forecasting*, Papers presented at the Eighty-Fifth Annual Meeting of the American Statistical Association, Washington D.C., December 27-29, 1923. Houghton-Mifflin, Boston.

Poole, W., 1970. Optimal Choice of Monetary Policy Instruments in a Simple Stochastic Macro Model. *Quarterly Journal of Economics*, 84(2), 197-216, May.

Razzak, W., 2003. Is the Taylor rule really different from the McCallum rule? *Contemporary Economic Policy*, forthcoming.

Reed, H., 1930. *Federal Reserve Policy, 1921-1930*, McGraw-Hill, New York.

Romer, C.D., Romer, D.H., 2000. Federal Reserve Information and the Behavior of Interest Rates. *American Economic Review*, 90(3), 429-457, June.

Romer, C.D., Romer, D.H., 2002. A Rehabilitation of Monetary Policy in the 1950s. *American Economic Review*, 92(2), 121-127, May.

Rotemberg, J.J., Woodford, M., 1999. Interest Rate Rules in an Estimated Sticky Price Model. In Taylor (1999).

Sack, B., Wieland, V., 2000. Interest-Rate Smoothing and Optimal Monetary Policy: A Review of Recent Empirical Evidence. *Journal of Economics and Business*, 52(1/2), 205-228, January/April.

Samuelson, P., 1951. Principles and Rules in Modern Fiscal Policy. Reprinted in Stiglitz (Ed.), 1966.

Samuelson, P., 1967. Stabilization Policies in the Contemporary U.S. Economy. In Horwich, 1967.

Snyder, C., 1923. A New Index of the Volume of Trade. *Journal of the American Statistical Association*, 18(144), 949-963, December 1923.

Sprague, O.M.W., 1921. The Discount Policy of the Federal Reserve Banks. *American Economic Review*, 11(1), 16-29, March.

Staiger, D., Stock, J.H., Watson, M.W., 1997. How Precise are Estimates of the Natural Rate of Unemployment? In *Reducing Inflation: Motivation and Strategy*, ed. by Christina D. Romer and David H. Romer, University of Chicago Press, Chicago, 195-246.

Stiglitz, J.E. (Ed.), 1966. *The Collected Scientific Papers of Paul A. Samuelson*, Volume II, MIT, Cambridge, MA.

Stock, J.H., Watson, M.W., 1993. *Business Cycles, Indicators, and Forecasting*, Chicago: University of Chicago Press.

Taylor, J.B., 1985. What would nominal GNP targeting do to the business cycle. Carnegie-Rochester conference series on Public Policy, 22, 61-84.

Taylor, J.B., 1993. Discretion versus Policy Rules in Practice. Carnegie-Rochester Conference Series on Public Policy, 39, December, 195-214.

Taylor, J.B., 1997. Policy Rules as a Means to Monetary Policy. In Kuroda, 1997.

Taylor, J.B. (Ed.), 1999. *Monetary Policy Rules*. University of Chicago, Chicago.

Taylor, J.B., 1999b. A Historical Analysis of Monetary Policy Rules. In Taylor, 1999.

Tobin, J., 1983. Monetary Policy: Rules, Targets and Shocks. *Journal of Money, Credit and Banking*, 15(4), 506-518, November.

United States Congress, 1957. *Investigation of the Financial Condition of the United States: Hearings before the Committee of Finance, United States Senate*. United States Government Printing Office, Washington DC.

United States Congress, 1927. *Stabilization: Hearings before the Committee on Banking and Currency, House of Representatives*. United States Government Printing Office, Washington DC.

United States Department of Commerce, 1958. Real National Output by Quarters—A New Major Economic Indicator. Survey of Current Business, December.

van Norden, S., 2002. Filtering for Current Analysis. Bank of Canada Working Paper 2002-28, October.

Walsh, C.E., 2003. Speed Limit Policies: The Output Gap and Optimal Monetary Policy. American Economic Review, 93(1), 265-278, March.

Williams, J.C., 1999. Simple Rules for Monetary Policy. Finance and Economics Discussion Series, 99-12, Board of Governors of the Federal Reserve System, February.

Woodford, M., 1999. Optimal Monetary Policy Inertia. NBER Working Paper 7261, July.

Woodford, M., 2002. *Interest and Prices: Foundations of a Theory of Monetary Policy*, in preparation for Princeton University Press.

Yohe, W.P., 1990. The Intellectual Milieu at the Federal Reserve Board in the 1920s. *History of Political Economy*, 22(3), 465-488.

Zarnowitz, V., Braun, P.A., 1993. Twenty-two Years of the NBER-ASA Quarterly Economic Surveys: Aspects and Comparisons of Forecasting Performance. In Stock and Watson (1993).

Table 1. Estimated Policy Rules

	θ_0	θ_i	θ_π	$\theta_{\Delta y}$	θ_y	see
Greenbook Forecasts						
1969:1–1997:4	−0.42	0.88	0.44	0.27	0.14	1.04
	(0.29)	(0.04)	(0.10)	(0.10)	(0.03)	
1969:1–1979:2	0.53	0.75	0.44	0.14	0.19	0.95
	(0.92)	(0.14)	(0.12)	(0.15)	(0.04)	
1982:3–1997:4	−0.33	0.81	0.52	0.51	0.10	0.56
	(0.32)	(0.06)	(0.13)	(0.17)	(0.03)	
Survey Forecasts						
1969:1–2002:4	−0.51	0.84	0.55	0.36	0.17	0.96
	(0.22)	(0.05)	(0.12)	(0.13)	(0.03)	
1969:1–1979:2	0.74	0.91	0.25	0.32	0.21	0.99
	(1.28)	(0.29)	(0.16)	(0.35)	(0.05)	
1982:3–2002:4	−0.66	0.83	0.58	0.53	0.16	0.49
	(0.21)	(0.05)	(0.09)	(0.11)	(0.03)	

Notes: Least squares estimates of:

$$i_t = \theta_0 + \theta_i i_{t-1} + \theta_\pi \pi^a_{t+3} + \theta_{\Delta y}\Delta^a y_{t+3} + \theta_y y_{t-1}$$

where $\pi^a_{t+3} = p_{t+3} - p_{t-1}$, $y_{t-1} = q_{t-1} - q^*_{t-1}$ and $\Delta^a y_{t+3} = y_{t+3} - y_{t-1} = \Delta^a q_{t+3} - \Delta^a q^*_{t+3}$
All variables dated t and later reflect real-time forecasts formed during quarter t. HAC standard errors in parentheses.

Figure 1. The U.S. Economy since the Accord

Inflation (Output Deflator)

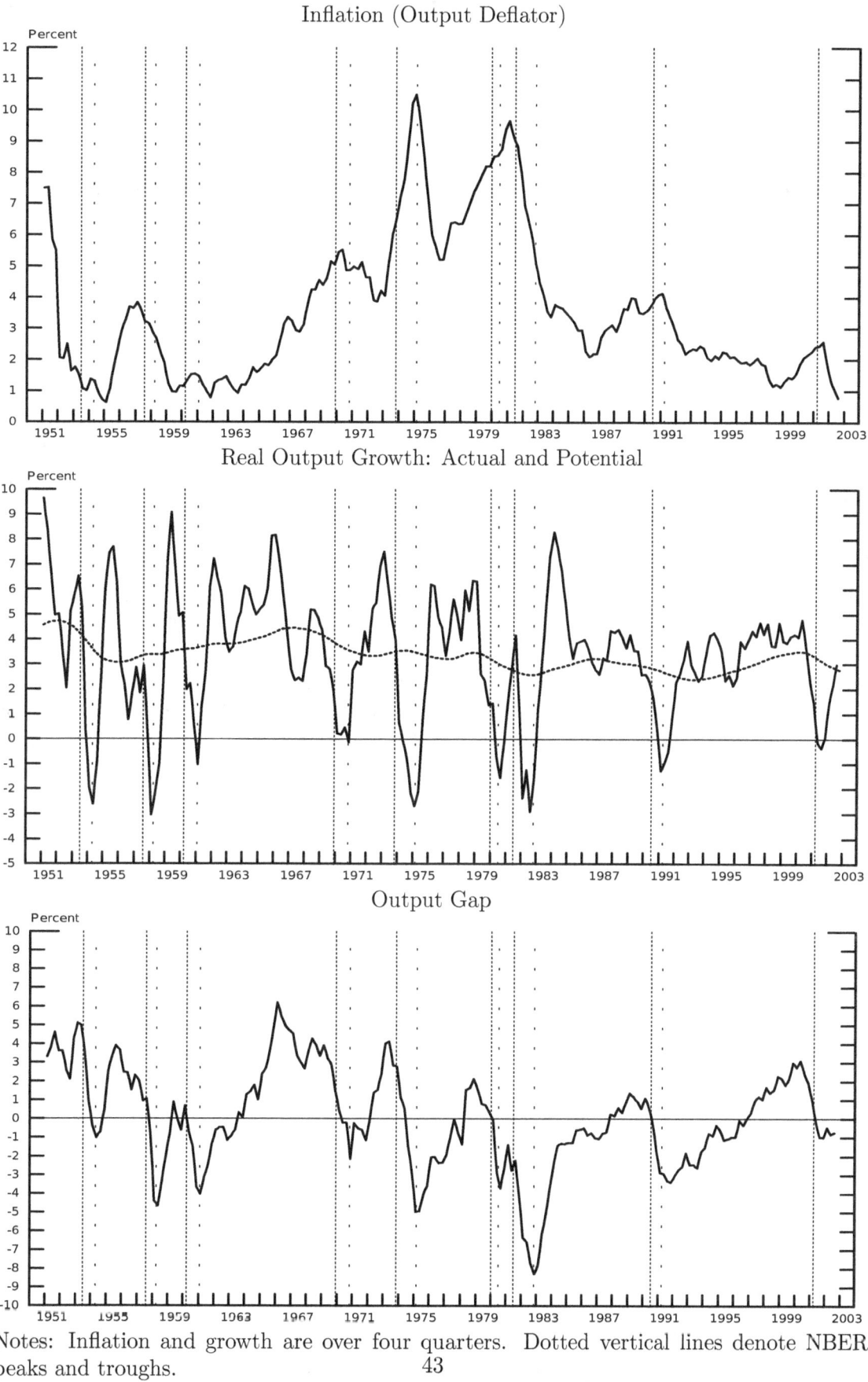

Real Output Growth: Actual and Potential

Output Gap

Notes: Inflation and growth are over four quarters. Dotted vertical lines denote NBER peaks and troughs.

Figure 2. The Classic Taylor Rule

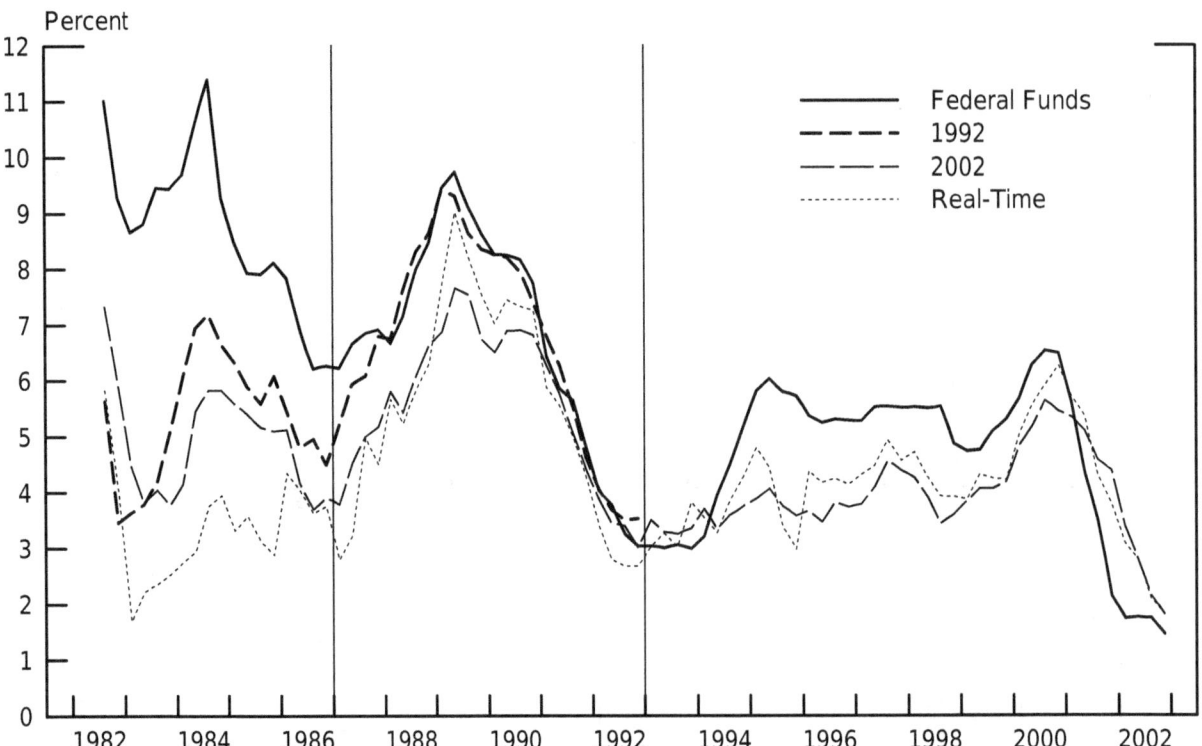

Notes: The 1992 rendition of the Taylor rule replicates the rule shown in Taylor (1993). The solid vertical lines show the beginning and end of the sample originally discussed in Taylor (1993). The 2002 rendition employs the latest data (Figure 1). The real-time rendition employs, in every quarter, data as available in that quarter (Figure 3).

Figure 3. Real-Time and Retrospective Views of the Economy

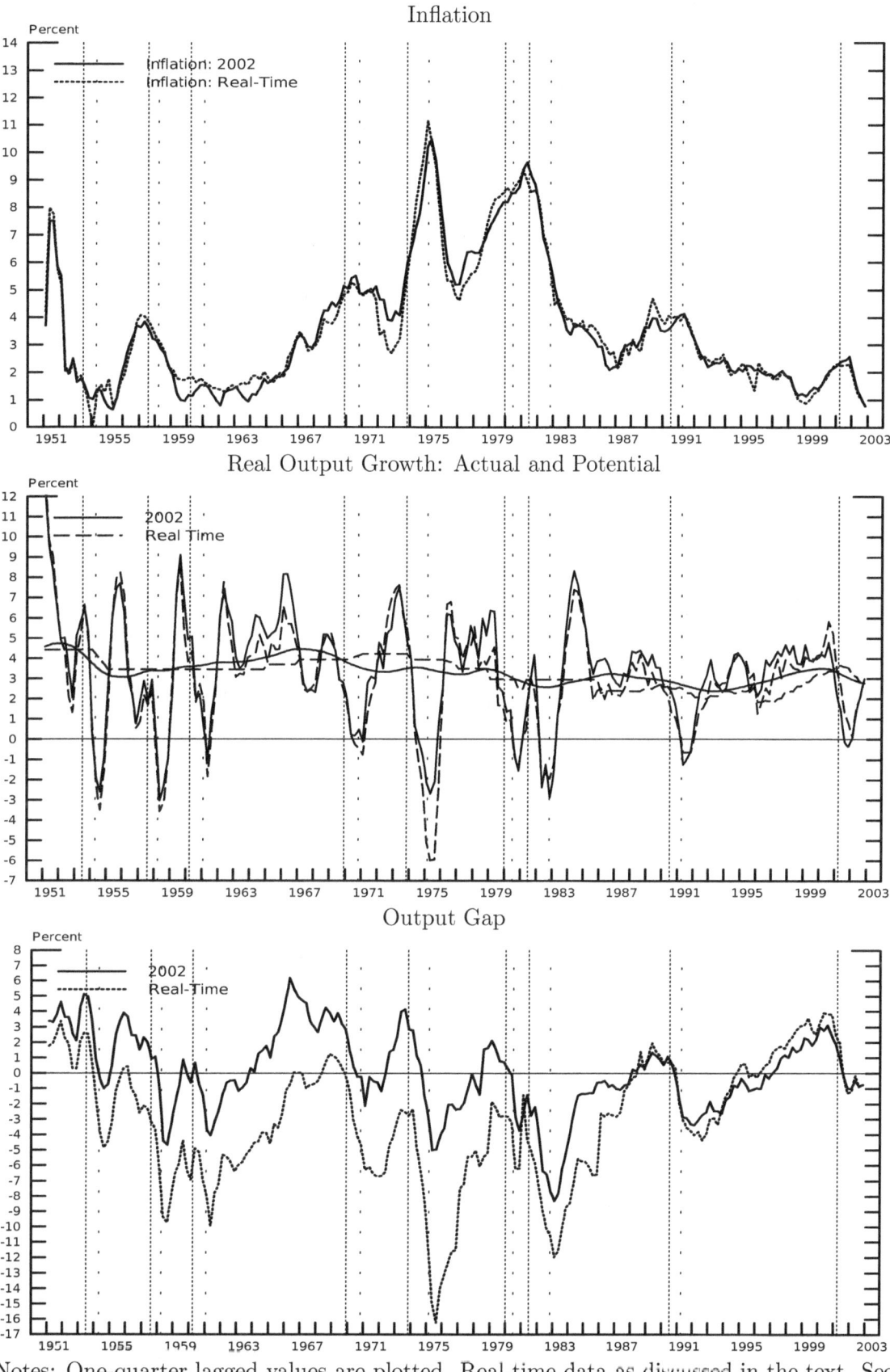

Inflation

Real Output Growth: Actual and Potential

Output Gap

Notes: One-quarter lagged values are plotted. Real-time data as discussed in the text. See also notes to Figure 1.

Figure 4. Real-Time and Retrospective Classic Taylor Rule

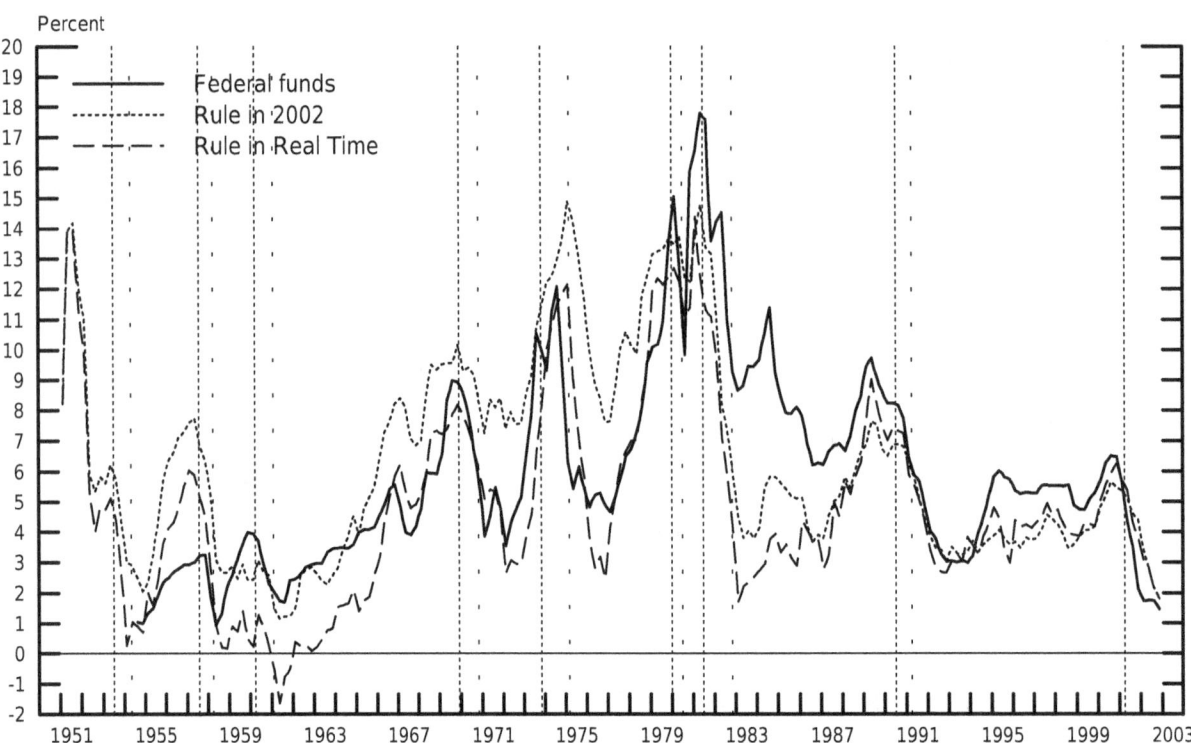

Notes: Real-time and retrospective renditions of the classic Taylor rule based on real-time and retrospective data shown in Figure 3. Dotted vertical lines denote NBER peaks and troughs.

Figure 5

Output Gap: Actual and Implied by Classic Rule

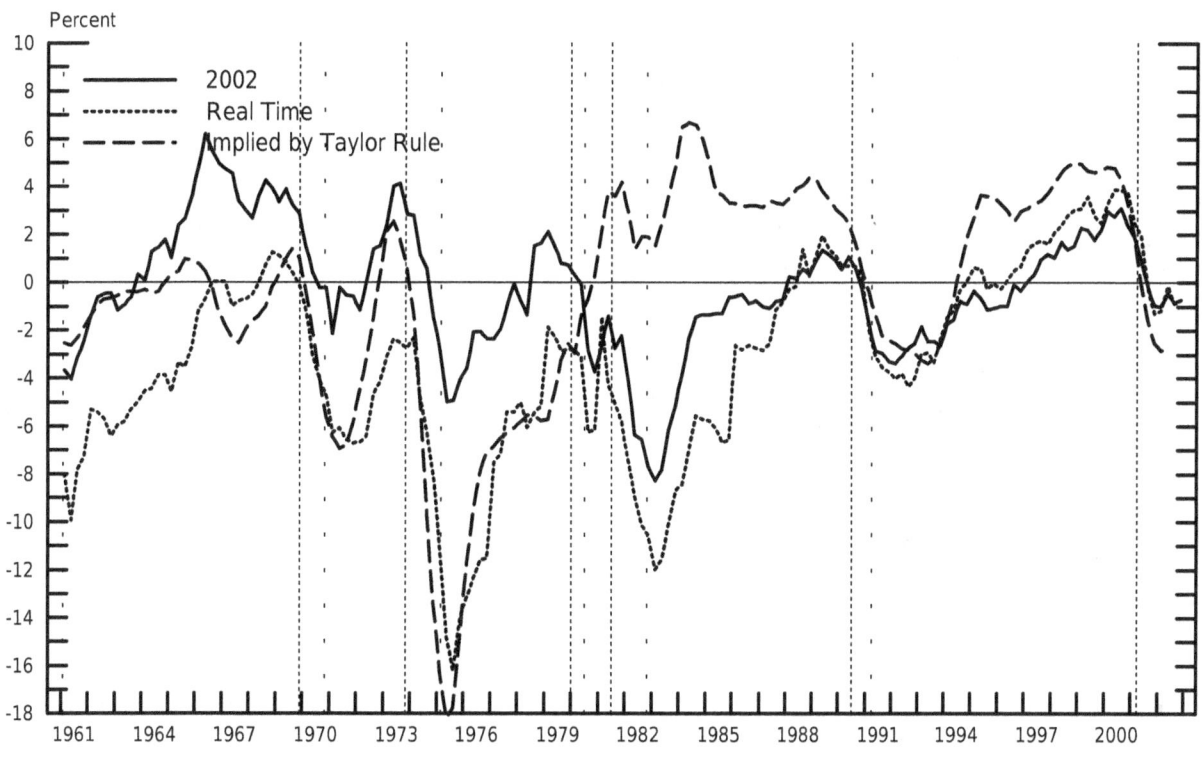

Evolution of Historical Output Gap Perceptions

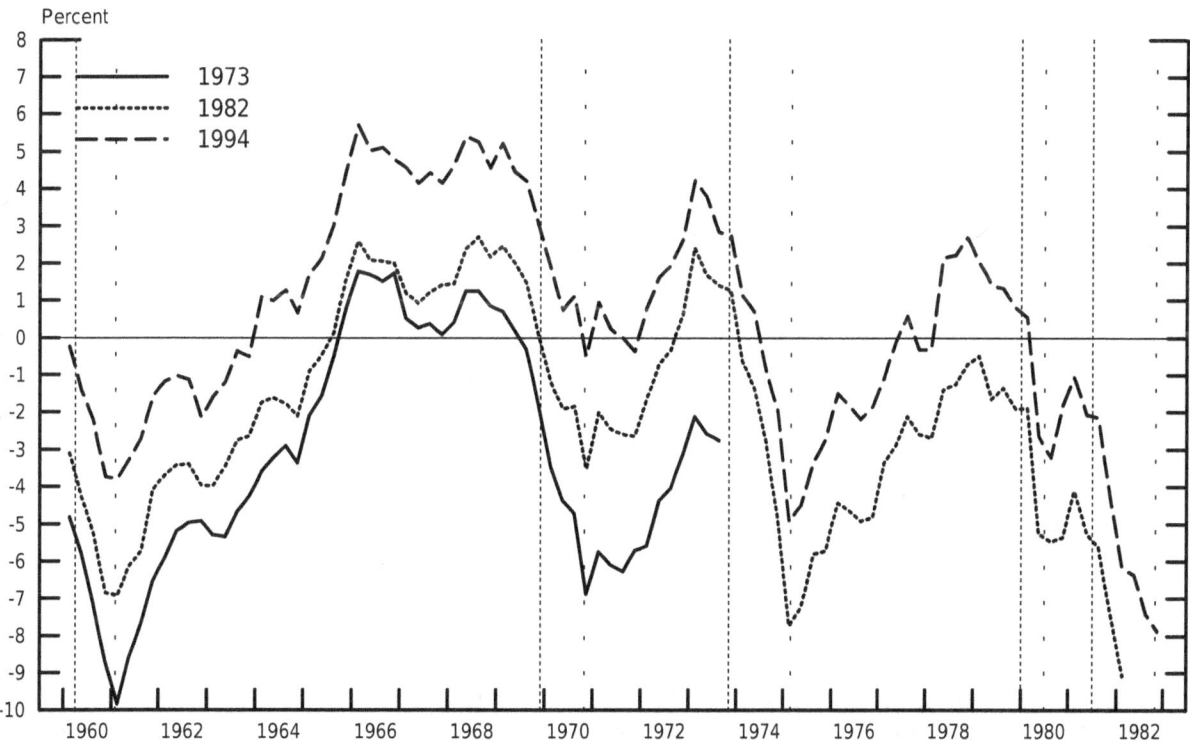

Figure 6

Forecast-Based Variants of the Classic Rule

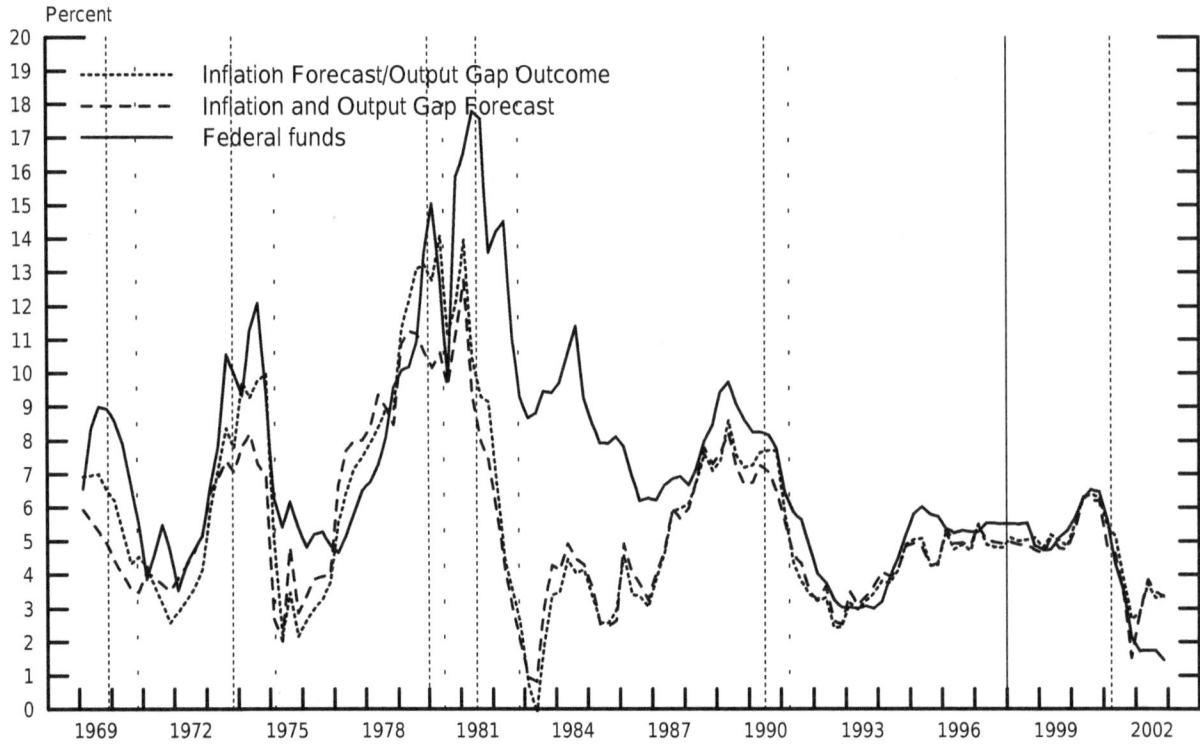

Classic and Forecast-Based Natural-Growth Rule

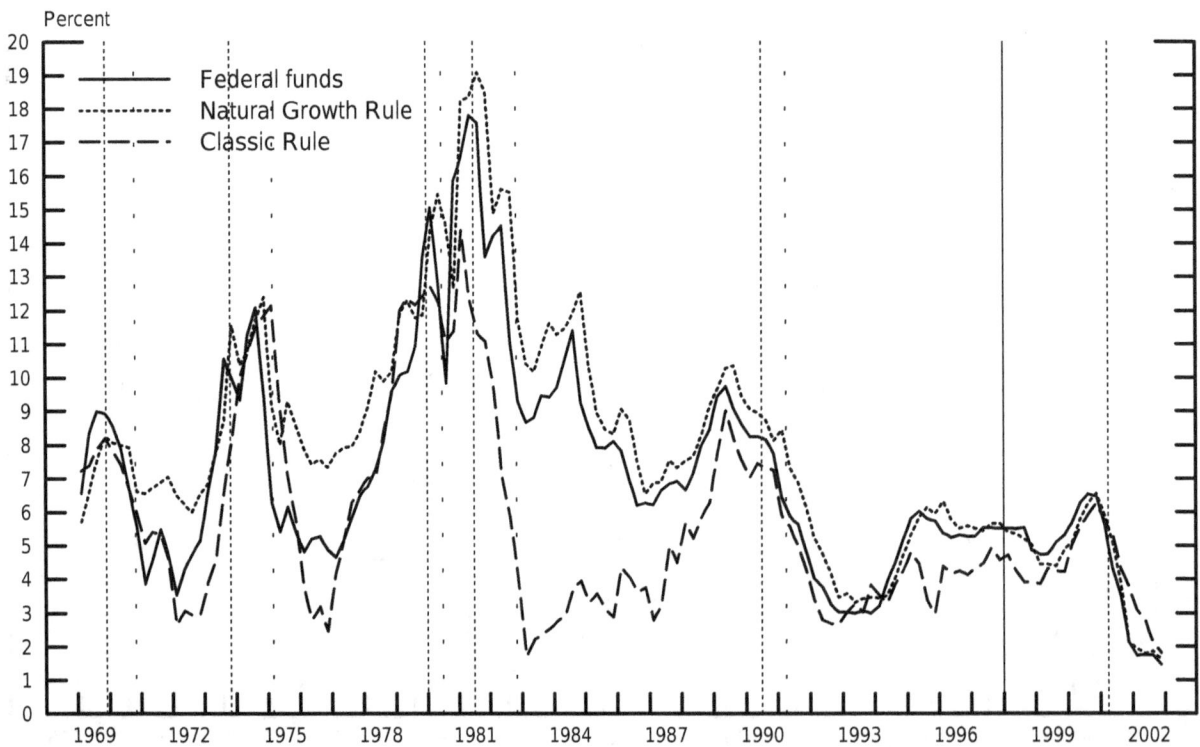

Notes: Forecasts are from the Greenbook until 1997Q4 and from the Survey of Professional Forecasters from 1998Q1 on. The solid vertical line indicates the break in the data source. Dotted vertical lines denote NBER peaks and troughs.

Figure 7. The High-Tide Years as a Prelude to the Crash

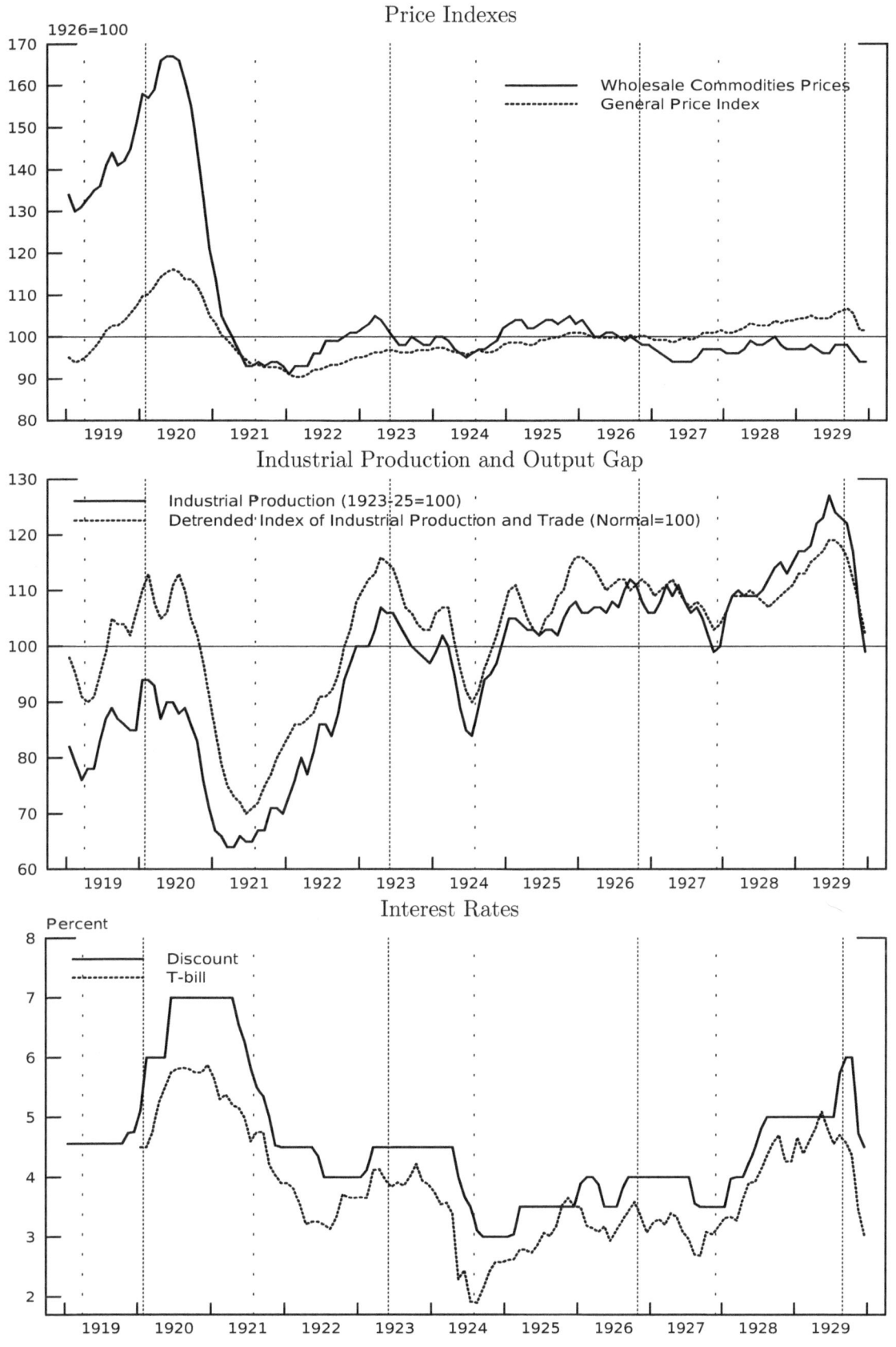

Price Indexes

Industrial Production and Output Gap

Interest Rates

49